POLICY FOR

Responding to children'

Adrian Voce

First published in Great Britain in 2015 by

Policy Press
University of Bristol
1-9 Old Park Hill
Bristol BS2 8BB
UK
t: +44 (0)117 954 5940
pp-info@bristol.ac.uk
www.policypress.co.uk

North American office:
Policy Press
c/o The University of Chicago Press
1427 East 60th Street
Chicago, IL 60637, USA
t: +1 773 702 7700
f: +1 773 702 9756
sales@press.uchicago.edu
www.press.uchicago.edu

© Policy Press 2015

British Library Cataloguing in Publication Data
A catalogue record for this book is available from the British Library.

Library of Congress Cataloging-in-Publication Data
A catalog record for this book has been requested.

ISBN 978-1-4473-1942-9 paperback
ISBN 978-1-4473-1944-3 ePub
ISBN 978-1-4473-1945-0 Kindle

Cover design by David Rodgers
Front cover: image kindly supplied by www.alamy.com
Printed and bound in Great Britain by CMP, Poole
The Policy Press uses environmentally responsible print partners

For Eran and Theo

Contents

Who's who

This section gives the names and roles of politicians, public figures and organisations (and their commonly used acronyms) featured in the text. Ministerial and shadow cabinet positions listed are those relevant to the individual's involvement in play policy.

4Children, *formerly National Out-of-School Alliance (NOOSA) then Kids Clubs Network:* national charity originally to support network of after-school clubs, later promoting policy for children and young people more generally; key government partner for the National Childcare Strategy.

Beverley Hughes MP (Labour): Minister for Children, Young People and Families (2005-9).

BIG, Big Lottery Fund: the major lottery distributor for the charitable sector, responsible for £200 million of children's play programmes across the UK from 2006-11.

Bright Blue: a policy think tank.

Children's Play Council (CPC) *formerly National Voluntary Council for Children's Play:* national alliance of non-commercial play organisations, under the aegis of the National Children's Bureau (NCB). Later evolved into Play England as a result of the Children's Play Initiative (2006-11).

Children's Play and Recreation Unit (CPRU): non-departmental government agency established within the Sports Council (1987) to take forward play policy after demise of Playboard.

Chris Smith MP, *later Lord Smith of Finsbury* **(Labour):** Secretary of State for Culture, Media and Sport (1997-2001).

Compass: a policy think tank.

David Cameron MP (Conservative): Prime Minister, 2010-15 and re-elected, 2015.

David Lammy MP (Labour): Minister for Culture, including children's play (2005-7).

David Willetts MP (Conservative): Shadow Secretary of State for Innovation, Universities and Skills (2007-9).

Department for Children, Schools and Families (DCSF): government department with joint responsibility for play policy (jointly with DCMS, 2008-10).

Department for Culture, Media and Sport (DCMS), *formerly Department for National Heritage*: government department with responsibility for play policy, 1982-2010 (jointly with DCSF, 2008-10).

Department for Education (DfE): restructured from former DCSF and divested of play policy, 2010.

Demos: a policy think tank.

Ed Balls MP (Labour): Secretary of State for Children, Schools and Families, 2007-10.

Frank Dobson MP (Labour): former Health Secretary and London Mayoral Candidate, longstanding chair of Coram's Fields Playground in Central London, chair of the national Play Review for England (2002-3).

Helen Goodman MP (Labour): chief executive of the National Association of Toy and Leisure Libraries (2002-5); chair of Children's Play Council (2005); Deputy Leader of the House of

Commons (2007-9); first chair of the All Party Parliamentary Group on Children's Play (2006-8).

Inner London Education Authority (ILEA): education authority for the inner London boroughs from 1965 until its abolition in 1990. Provided financial support, via LAPA, for adventure playgrounds in those boroughs

Ken Livingstone (Independent/Labour): first elected Mayor of London (2000-8).

Lady Allen of Hurtwood (Marjory Allen, née Gill): landscape architect and pioneering play advocate; champion of adventure playgrounds (she is credited with coining the term), play for disabled children and strategic planning for play in urban areas (d.1972).

London Adventure Playground Association (LAPA), *later known as PLAYLINK:* London charity formed to support, advocate and develop good practice for the city's voluntary managed adventure playgrounds (1962-99; thereafter, PLAYLINK continued as an independent consultancy).

London Play: regional play charity established in 1998; worked with Mayor of London to develop play policy for the city.

Margaret Hodge MP (Labour): Minister for Children, Young People and Families (2003-5).

National Playing Fields Association (NPFA), *later known as Fields in Trust:* national charity for outdoor sport, play and recreation, founded in 1925. Creator of the Six-Acre Standard. Held central government contracts for play during the 1990s.

New Opportunities Fund (NOF): National Lottery distributor under broad ministerial policy direction (1999-2004). Merged with the Community Fund to form the Big Lottery Fund (BIG) in 2004-5.

Nick Clegg MP (Liberal Democrat): Deputy Prime Minister, 2010-15.

Play England, *formerly the Children's Play Council*: national play charity for England, established at National Children's Bureau (NCB) in 2006. Independent since 2014. Simultaneously held the main government contracts for the Play Strategy (2008-10) and a strategic grant from the Big Lottery Fund (BIG) to support the Children's Play Initiative (2006-11).

Playboard (Association for Children's Play and Recreation): short-lived (1982-7) national body for play; recipient of first UK government contract solely for children's play.

PLAYLINK, *formerly LAPA*: charity for play research and policy advocacy, later an independent play consultancy.

Skillsactive, *formerly Sprito*: government-licenced Sector Skills Council for occupations in sport and recreation, including playwork.

Sprito, *later Skillsactive*: National Training Organisation for sports and recreation.

Stephen Dunmore: Chief Executive of the New Opportunities Fund (2001-5) and the Big Lottery Fund (2005-9).

Tim Loughton MP (Conservative): Shadow Children's Minister (2003-10), Minister for Children and Families (2010-12).

United Nations Committee on the Rights Of The Child: Council of the United Nations responsible for the Convention on the Rights of the Child (CRC) and its later General Comment 17 (GC17) on Article 31 of the convention, which covers children's right to play.

United Nations Convention on the Rights of the Child (CRC or UNCRC): The international human rights treaty that grants all children and young people a comprehensive set of rights. UK government policies and practices must comply with the CRC, which the government signed in 1990 and ratified in 1991.

United Nations General Comment 17 on Article 31 of the CRC (GC17): United Nations statement issued in 2013, explicating and elaborating on states' obligations to meet children's right to rest and leisure, to engage in play and recreational activities and to participate freely in cultural life and the arts; commonly known simply as 'the right to play'.

About the author

Adrian Voce was a playworker and inclusive play trainer before becoming the first director of the charity London Play, where he helped to develop a play policy for the city, working with the Mayor of London.

He was then appointed director of the national Children's Play Council – after first serving as its chair – where he founded Play England to lead the campaign and provide the support for a national government play strategy. Together with the lottery programme that preceded it, this saw more than £360 million of public funding invested over five years in developing and improving provision for school-age children's play in England.

Now a writer and consultant, Adrian also serves on the board of the European Child in the City Foundation, and is involved in the development of a new not-for-profit vehicle for playwork.

In his various roles he has commissioned, drafted and edited a number of publications on research, policy, planning and provision for children's play. This is his first book as an independent author.

In 2011, Adrian was awarded an OBE for services to children.

Preface

When I embarked on this project, I was keenly aware that my credentials for writing the book were solely based on personal experience. Policy Press wanted the story of the Play Strategy for England of 2008-10. I was as able as anyone to tell it, and believed it needed to be told.

But the Play Strategy was just one policy response to children's 'forgotten right' and the original intention was to compare and contrast it to others, by other governments in different countries. However, I have discovered that what makes me (perhaps) well-qualified to write about English policy for play equally renders me an unsuitable chronicler of parallel events elsewhere. I am no historian, or any kind of academic. Even if I were, there was neither the time in the schedule nor space in the book to capture such a broad subject sufficiently to do it justice. I have therefore left the equivalent stories from the devolved UK and elsewhere to others.

However, one of those developments in particular must be noted here, if only to urge the reader to further research. In 2002, the devolved Welsh Government adopted a children's rights approach to policy formulation that included an unprecedented national government play policy (Welsh Assembly Government,[1] 2002). This led, over time, to a statutory duty on local authorities to assess and secure sufficient play opportunities for children in their area: probably the first such requirement anywhere in the world.

The Welsh play policy continues to inspire hope for play advocates everywhere. The continuity of government there seems to have protected it, so far, from the reversal that happened in England in 2010. The vibrant Welsh play and playwork sector is busy supporting its implementation and exploring ways to effectively evaluate its

---

[1] The Welsh Assembly Government changed its name to Welsh Government in May 2011.

impact. Perhaps someone from Play Wales[2] will one day write its story. Equally, some positive play policy developments in Scotland, Northern Ireland and other parts of the world are best related by advocates from the relevant countries.

Another area not covered much by the book is the question of play in schools and in early years provision. The Play Strategy only touched on these domains peripherally and they are not my area of experience, although the implications for education, early years' and childcare policy of a more enlightened approach to children's play – one based on the trans-disciplinary perspectives touched on in the book – would seem to be considerable. That, however, is another book.

As far as this one is concerned, I must thank Mick Conway, Morgan Leichter-Saxby and Darijana Hahn for their helpful comments on the first draft; Roger Hart for his perfect foreword and for his encouraging comments on the manuscript; Anna Kassman-McKerrell for her valuable help during the final days of the Children's Play Information Service in London; Isobel Bainton and Rebecca Tomlinson at Policy Press for their support (and patience); and the hundreds of amazing playwork friends and colleagues who have shared the journey with me and who tread the path still, bloodied but undaunted.

Mostly, I want to thank my wife, Jacqui Penalver for her love and support; for allowing me the time and space to write; and for believing that I could.

Adrian Voce
May 2015

---

[2] The national charity for children's right to play in Wales, and the leading advocate for Welsh Government play policy.

Foreword

Roger Hart

*Center for Human Environments and the Children's Environments
Research Group, City University of New York*

This book needed to be written.

As well as providing a road map for all who want England to again move forward in improving everyday play opportunities for children, it will also become a key resource for play advocates and policymakers everywhere, offering a template for effective, long-term government action in this neglected but crucial area of public life.

Like all countries in the industrialised world, England has been suffering in recent decades from a great erosion of children's mobility, and a diminution of their freedom to play. While there are many overlapping forces that have led to this state of affairs, there is much that can be done to ameliorate or even reverse the trend.

What follows is a remarkable account of the campaign to develop a national policy and commitment in England to do just that. By offering a detailed chronological account of these efforts, during the recent decades of significant social, economic and political change in the UK, it offers a unique window into the complex set of forces that influence whether children's play is taken for granted, directed and interrupted, or allowed to flourish. The book bases its forceful arguments for play policy on a thoroughly convincing explanation of children's right to play, and its crucial importance for both their 'here-and-now' lives as children and for their longer-term development and well-being.

Much of the book's wonderful evocation of why play is central to being a child comes from the field of *playwork* – the uniquely British profession that understands children's daily lives out of school

– their play, their culture and the spaces that best afford it – better than any other. The author, a playworker himself, gives full voice to the central role of this young profession as a guiding force for change, not only in the play lives of the children who access its services, but also within the spheres of public life where debates are enjoined and policy made. He is clear that a key part of playwork is advocacy: for play, and for policy for play.

In a world where the dominant discourse in so much of child policy, and the theories underpinning it, is about ever-increasing the effectiveness of services and interventions – whether in education, health or social care – on children's future 'life chances' (usually measured in their projected economic performance as adults), the public, as well as policymakers, could learn much from the playwork approach. In the face of enormous changes in conditions for children we need more than ever adults who are sensitively attuned to them. Playworkers are trained to reflect and respond to the worlds of children rather than presuming to educate them to ours. Placing themselves solely at the service of children's play and how best to support it, they listen to, respect and respond to children and young people on their own terms in a way that is too rare in public life, to the detriment of all of us.

The author describes the important decision to use the United Nations Convention on the Rights of the Child (CRC) as the framework for building a national play policy and strategy. But he is right to look critically at how the CRC has often been interpreted. He makes some important observations that require serious reflection by government and non-government organisations, on the tendency to overly focus on children's right to be heard as the primary means of fulfilling all their rights. The children's participation movement, in the UK and elsewhere, over the past three decades, has leaned heavily on formal consultation processes with select groups of children. Meanwhile, the erosion of all children's freedom to play and the ubiquitous everyday threats to their informal participation in the life of their own communities – the freedom to play with their friends in the common spaces of their neighbourhoods – calls for a much broader view of how to address children's rights.

The book points to the landmark decision by the Welsh Government in 2008 to place a legal duty on local authorities to assess and secure sufficient play opportunities for children throughout the spaces of their neighbourhoods, not just in playgrounds. The author is right to call on other governments to follow suit.

The book is a clarion call for English policymakers to re-engage with the pioneering national Play Strategy (2008-10), a bold ten-year plan that was cut short, in the wake of the economic crisis, after only two years. It will take a renewed multi-departmental government effort with civil society to create the conditions in all of the settings of children's daily lives for them to be able to play and socialise with their peers as much, and as freely, as they need and deserve. The journey will not be so difficult, for much of the path has already been trodden – and we now have the map!

As I write these words from the other side of the Atlantic, I reflect on how we in the US seem to be such a relatively small number who champion children's right to play. But now that the public and the media in the US are increasingly observing the deterioration of play opportunities, England, and the rest of the UK, is seen as a beacon of enlightened good practice, where an entire movement of play advocates, evolved and matured over decades, has shaped the national debate and moulded public policy. While US public officials have so far given little or no indication that provision for children's play is something worth thinking about, the battle lines are being drawn over the increasing control of children's time, through the promotion of hyper-competitive school instruction and a regime of testing, the removal of school play time and the addition of after-school schooling programming. This account of the UK play movement's impressive record of countering this and the other threats to children's play, by working with government to develop national policy, will provide inspiration for play advocates in the US, and no doubt in other countries.

Perhaps because it seems oxymoronic, the term 'playwork' can be sometimes poorly construed by the uninitiated. When I first introduced the profession to New York City (with the help of English playworkers) there was a great flood of negative public reaction, with a *New York Times* lead article assuming that this was a further encroachment of over-controlling adults into the child's domain, which of course could not be further from the truth. It's a continuing struggle for me to convince writers and the general public that opportunities for children to have the freedom to play and to self-organise in inclusive, non-segregated spaces with friendly adults nearby but not directing them is valuable to children and to the society. It is a key argument for the importance of maintaining safe and inviting public spaces for the building of an inclusive civil society in the face of increasing threats from commercial play provision and the privatisation of public space.

The story of England's play strategy – and the parallel development in Wales – has the potential to be a valuable springboard for a more enlightened engagement with the issue by the general public, as well as policymakers. My big hope is that it will help to revitalise the play movement in its challenge to bring the vital importance of children's play – and the concept of playwork – to a wider audience; contributing, ultimately, to a better understanding of children and their play, and to a public realm that supports and is enriched by it.

This book relates a unique development in public policy that, had it not coincided with the onset of the sharpest recession since the 1930s, would have seen a major western government take concerted long-term action to support all children and young people; not to do better in school, get fit, be safe, stay out of trouble or become good citizens – although it would have undoubtedly contributed to each of these outcomes – but to enjoy their lives as children now, re-inhabiting the common spaces from where they have become largely absent, filling their communities with the colour and vibrancy of their play.

It is a story, and a policy, we cannot afford to neglect.

Prologue

In a typical English residential street of Victorian terraced houses either side of a road, usually lined bumper to bumper with parked cars, children are playing in the manner of children everywhere: noisily; randomly; in small groups, pairs or just on their own.

Play perennials like skipping, hula hoops and hopscotch abound, although other games in evidence are more specific to this generation of children, this neighbourhood or this moment. Bikes, scooters and roller blades are in ample evidence but there are still more children on foot, though rarely walking. Running, skipping and jumping – or a combination of all three – seem to be the default modes of movement, leading nowhere in particular but full of intent.

The play seems infinitely varied, spontaneous and freeform. Although some adults are present, they are not in charge; no one is coordinating or directing save for the children themselves, who seem to be entirely at home in the happy chaos of it all. Much of the anarchic activity is happening in the middle of the road, the pavement being far too narrow to contain it all.

It is summer and at one end of the street someone has brought out a hose. Children are screaming with delight as they try – but not too hard – to evade the water's cold, wet arcs. Others are having a race, which is fiercely competitive but none too organised. There is little agreement about the winner, but no one seems to care much – or not for long anyway.

Such a scene, one might imagine, is commonplace. A normal day, perhaps a weekend, a school holiday or an early summer evening, in a normal street where families live and children gravitate towards one another in the one common space that is within sufficiently easy reach of their homes that they can come and go at will.

But look again, as we zoom out from this picture. There are no children playing in the adjacent street, or any of those parallel to it, though they house roughly the same demographic. Zoom back in and notice that at either end of the street are adults in 'high-vis' jackets wearing badges and holding clipboards. They have erected barriers and are keeping out traffic, apart from the occasional resident's vehicle, which is escorted at walking pace by one of these voluntary stewards.

For today is a 'street play day'. Tomorrow, the barriers will be gone and the cars will be back. Once again, many of these children wanting to play will be confined to their homes, looking for their fun from a screen.

INTRODUCTION

'To respect, protect and fulfil'

One weekday morning in the summer of 2004, over a hurried breakfast before joining the daily rush of London's commuter throng, along with an estimated audience of around nine million other radio listeners I tuned in to the *Today* programme on the BBC.

The Shadow Chancellor, Oliver Letwin MP (2004) of the Conservative Party, was being interviewed about one of his favourite themes in the run up to the following year's general election. This was how a new Tory administration would reduce taxes, not by cutting front line public services, but by reducing 'wasteful' expenditure on the 'fat bureaucracy' of government. Searching for an example to best illustrate the Labour government's alleged profligacy, he remarked that among the 'huge number of quangos' employing 'armies of bureaucrats' the government '*even has a council for children's play*'.

As the chair (shortly to become director) of the very same Children's Play Council (CPC), this sideswipe from the would-be Chancellor of the Exchequer was not what I was accustomed to hearing over breakfast. It was not just the dismissive nature of the remark that caught me off guard. The mere mention of children's play on the *Today* programme, let alone in a discussion of economic policy by a senior politician, was in itself enough of a surprise to cause our then-director, Tim Gill (2008a), to later confess to nearly choking on his toast.

CPC was not, in fact, a government agency or 'quango',[1] but a membership body of voluntary and public play organisations hosted by the National Children's Bureau (NCB), a registered charity. Although we did hold a small government contract, we were also funded by various charitable trusts and membership fees. Our role was very much that of an independent advocate for children's right to play. Researching and disseminating evidence about play and play provision, CPC's main aim was to build a consensus about how society in general, and government in particular, should respond to what we knew were increasing barriers to children's natural enjoyment of this fundamentally important part of their lives.

After checking with colleagues that we had no particular engagement with Letwin's office, let alone of the kind that might invoke such disapproval, we quickly came to realise that we had been singled out, not for anything we had said or done, but for what we represented to a particular school of thought. New Labour's supposed addiction to needless administration and its consequent failure, in Conservative eyes, to curb public expenditure, must be extreme indeed, Letwin had implied, for it to need a body concerned with something as trivial and inessential as children's play. He clearly hoped the voting public would be equally appalled.

Tim Gill (2008b) would later wryly observe that we had become a 'political football', a minor potential victim of collateral damage, insignificant and therefore expendable in the cut and thrust between the big parties. Nevertheless, this was more attention than we were used to receiving from the political class and, while presenting an opportunity to engage with one of the Conservatives' leading policymakers (who later granted us a meeting), the manner of it threw into sharp relief just what we were up against.

Leaving aside that the Shadow Chancellor had incorrectly identified CPC as part of a 'bloated' public bureaucracy, the incident is revealing for what it says about attitudes to children's play. Play is not something that most people, politicians or otherwise, associate with government policy, or even consider to be an issue at all. Its strong association with the concerns *of* children – as distinct from

---

[1] Quasi autonomous non-governmental organisation, sometimes referred to as non-departmental public bodies (NDPBs); that is, government-sponsored agencies not under the direct control of ministers.

concerns *about* children – tend to cause it to be viewed as frivolous and unimportant: 'child's play'. Its commonplace, ubiquitous nature means that even when its value is acknowledged, without its advocates play tends to be taken for granted as something that simply happens, regardless of context. It is generally considered as either not a policy matter or as something that can be commandeered to supposedly more important objectives, such as improving children's academic attainment, increasing their physical activity or engaging them in 'positive activities'.

While the precise nature of play remains elusive and indefinable (Sutton-Smith, 1997; Fagen, 2011), several academic disciplines – from evolutionary biology (Burghardt, 2005) to developmental psychology (Pellegrini et al, 2006) and the emergent neurosciences (Spinka et al, 2001) – agree in their different ways that children's play is central to who and what we are. Anthropological studies (Schwartzman, 1978) have similarly placed the play of children at the heart of human culture, community and society.

It seems clear from these various studies that playing has a vitally important role, both in individual development and in human evolution, but that its primary purpose is simply to be enjoyed. The great play scholar Brian Sutton-Smith (1999) famously said, 'the opposite of play isn't work. It's depression'; and the act of playing brings about 'renewed belief in the worthwhileness of merely living'.

Playing is children's default setting. After being fed, clothed, rested and feeling reasonably secure, their first need is to play. It is a deep biological and psychological trait found in virtually all animal species. It is the way that the young orientate themselves and discover how to engage with, navigate and co-create the world of which they are a part. For children, playing is the main medium for self-exploration and self-expression. They first form their self-identity by instinctively rehearsing and developing their emotional and physical repertoires through play. It is how they first encounter and learn to manage risks.

First and foremost, for children, play is fun. This compels them to seek opportunities for it in all circumstances and contexts. It is an evolutionary imperative, which means that playing children are acquiring the self-confidence and developing the mental and emotional capacity and adaptability to not only deal with what life might have in store for them, but also to live it fully, moment to playful moment. Children's capacity to create such moments is perhaps the only definition of their resilience that we need (Lester and Russell, 2013).

That children seek opportunities to play wherever and whenever they can should tell us something; but the vital role of play in child development is often widely misunderstood by policymakers, who can frequently be heard to say – as they contrive to manipulate and direct the play of children towards the acquisition of narrowly defined knowledge and skills – that there is no difference between play and learning. This dangerously misses the central point about playing, which is that children do it simply because they need to; because it is in their nature. Learning is incidental, unless it is to become better at the game (Sutton-Smith, 1997). Thus the structured, 'teacher-led play' in pursuit of specific learning goals – favoured, for example, by the UK government of 2010-15 (Truss, 2013) – is a contradiction in terms, and is not really playing at all.

To play the way that their biological instincts demand, children need space: cultural, social and emotional as well as physical and geographical space. That is, they need spacious environments that afford play opportunities, and they need permission and confidence to use them without the encroachment of adult agendas.

Because the need for play is universal (Barkow et al, 1992) – albeit not uniformly manifest (Roopnarine, 2011) – it follows that these environments must be part of the public realm, accessible and available to all children; but play's self-directed nature (Cornell et al, cited in Lester and Maudsley, 2006) and practically infinite variability (Sutton-Smith, 1997) calls for a different type of public realm from that which has increasingly become the minority[2] world norm (Jacobs, 1961; Beunderman et al, 2007). Children need a degree of freedom that is now only rarely granted to them. Space to play is increasingly controlled, dominated or narrowly prescribed to children by adult society (Morrow, 2004). By a range of measures, the space and opportunity for children to play is diminishing (Thomas and Hocking, 2003; UNICEF, 2007).

The scene depicted in the prologue was not, of course, of a typical street on a normal day. Most pre-teen children in modern

---

[2]   'Minority world' is a term used within a number of academic disciplines to describe what has been more commonly called either the Western or the new world.

Britain do not often 'play out' in their local neighbourhoods (Lacey, 2007). Their independent mobility or 'licence' to come and go unaccompanied was drastically curtailed during the latter quarter of the twentieth century (Hillman et al, 1990) and does not appear to be recovering (Karsten and Van Vliet, 2006). It is widely considered dangerous, socially unacceptable or both for children to be outside without adults (Lacey, 2007). Mostly, during out-of-school hours, they are either inside – doing their homework, watching TV, playing Minecraft, chatting on Facebook – or out somewhere with adults: shopping perhaps, or at the leisure centre, in an after-school club, having private lessons or maybe at the park or local playground (Gleave, 2009). In each case, they are by and large closely supervised.

No, the children in our opening scene are not so much playing out as 'Playing Out': participants in a project organised by adults so that their children could 'have some of the same sorts of freedom we had when we were kids, to play outside' (Ferguson, 2011). It will run for a few hours and then the barriers will come down, the hi-vis jackets removed, the traffic free again to assume right of way. The children will be taken back inside or into the car and on to the next structured activity, until the next time the council grants them permission to enjoy their community space without the real risk of death or injury from traffic[3] or the perceived threat of predatory strangers.[4]

In years gone by such scenes, without the barriers or the stewards, were indeed commonplace. Throughout human history, until very recently, children have tended to play – and had the freedom to play – in the streets where they lived, or the equivalent common spaces between and around their dwellings (Lacey, 2007).

But this is 2015, and without projects like Playing Out, organised and promoted by local parents who know what is being lost, 'free-range kids' (Skenazy, 2009) are disappearing from public space – have indeed disappeared altogether from many places, certainly in

---

[3] 'Around 5,000 children under the age of 16 die or are seriously injured on Britain's roads each year. Nearly two in three road accidents happen when children are walking or playing' (AA Motoring Trust, 2014).

[4] 'Over four-fifths of completed abductions recorded by the police involve a perpetrator known to the victim. Less than one-fifth are committed by a stranger' (Newiss and Traynor, 2013).

their primary school years. This is the age of the 'battery-reared child' (Gill, 2004) in which the play of children – which has been a fundamental, instinctive part of the human story, integral to our evolution (Pellegrini et al, 2006) – is being confined and constrained like never before.

This change – which many experts, including the government's own (Chief Medical Officer, 2013) believe has profound implications for children's health (Dietz, 2001) and development (Gray, 2015), as well as the nature of society itself (Louv, 2005) – is neither inevitable nor irreversible but rather a result of decisions about how we conceive, design, develop and manage public space and public services and how they each respond to children; and the extent to which these decisions are made by governments in the public interest for the common good, or not (Meek, 2015).

This book is about how governments can tackle this issue and explores the case for why it should be much more of a priority that they do. It is also about how in England, local, regional and national governments seriously embarked on a long-term plan to halt and reverse this trend before the coalition government of 2010-15 abandoned the policy in the name of economic prudence in response to the great financial crash of 2007-8.

The right to play is recognised in international law under Article 31 of the United Nations Convention on the Rights of the Child (CRC) of 1989, the most widely agreed global treaty in history. Article 31 of the CRC obliges its parties to 'recognise the right of the child to rest and leisure, to engage in play and recreational activities appropriate to the age of the child and to participate freely in cultural life and the arts' (United Nations Office of the High Commissioner for Human Rights, 1989).

In April 2013, the UN issued a General Comment[5] (GC17) on Article 31 (Committee on the Rights of the Child, 2013) expanding on the responsibilities that it places on nation states and urging them 'to elaborate measures to ensure' its full implementation. GC17 makes it clear that, in the face of increasing barriers, the UN expects national governments to honour its obligations to 'respect, protect

---

[5] A UN General Comment is defined as 'the interpretation of the provisions of (its) respective human rights treaty' by its treaty bodies. In other words, it is the UN's own interpretation of how nation states should meet their obligations under international law.

and fulfil' children's right to play by taking serious and concerted action on a range of fronts including, in particular, 'legislation, planning and funding'. The UN hoped that GC17 would 'raise the profile, awareness and understanding [...] of the centrality of the right to play' (Committee on the Rights of the Child, 2013). On its publication, children's rights advocates did indeed hail it as a landmark document. The four UK Children's Commissioners, for example, made the following statement:

> We are [now] calling on the UK Government and the respective governments of Scotland, Northern Ireland and Wales to fulfil their duty to respect, protect and fulfil Article 31 and understand that its implementation and realisation will contribute to helping each and every child, whatever their circumstance, to reach their full potential, not only in relation to individual growth but also as competent and full members of society.

These remarks were widely echoed by play campaigners such as those of the International Association for the Child's Right to Play (IPA, 2013), which had worked for many years to help develop the UN's position on Article 31.

However, while IPA and the children's commissioners may have hailed the General Comment as a 'landmark moment for children' (Casey and McConaghy, 2014), the world at large seemed unmoved. The UK news at the time was dominated by stories and comment about the death of the former Prime Minister, Margaret Thatcher, and her legacy. It is unlikely, however, that a quieter news week would have found space for it either. Rarely high on the policy agenda, children's rights in general and children's play in particular commanded even less attention than usual during the years of fiscal austerity that followed the financial crash of 2007–8. The event passed without remark by the UK government or the mainstream British media.

If this indifference to the UN's newly expansive interpretation of Article 31 were not evidence enough of its attitude to children's play, the UK government's report (HM Government, 2014) the following year on its progress in implementing the CRC gave further indication of how seriously it took its obligations under article 31. Even under the section headed 'Right to Leisure and Play', the perceived unimportance of play is immediately brought home by the opening sentence: 'there is a firm principle across the UK that all children should be able to enjoy and participate in culture, sports and leisure' (HM Government, 2014). The 86-page document, covering the actions of each of the four different national UK administrations, then carries only three cursory paragraphs (HM Government, 2014) on a play policy long since abandoned, with no reference to future plans.

Such disregard of the child's right to play by government and its agencies has been so common that it has become known in advocacy circles as children's 'forgotten right' (IPA, 2013). Yet between Oliver Letwin's remarks on the *Today* programme in 2004 and the formation of a new coalition government by the Conservatives and the Liberal Democrats in 2010 there occurred a period of social policy in the UK, under Labour governments for England and Wales in particular, that markedly bucked this trend. Had it not been for the extraordinary measures of the coalition to reduce the scale and scope of the public sector immediately on taking office, this period of social policy would in all probability have demonstrated a full implementation of Article 31 for the UN to hold up as an example.

There is a perennial debate between play advocates about the relative merits of rights-based and evidence-based approaches to influencing and developing policy. These will be explored in the book, but our starting point is that the CRC is a charter for the human rights of children everywhere, which the nations of the world have agreed almost without exception. Children in their own right cannot hold governments to account for honouring this agreement. They do not even have the vote. According to the UN Committee on the Rights of the Child, it therefore falls to their advocates 'to insist on it' (Krappmann, 2011).

The book therefore aims not simply to consider the implications of Article 31 and GC17 as an international charter for children's play, or indeed merely a hypothetical framework for play policy, but to explore, through a detailed case study of what was achieved, especially in England, where there was a 12-year strategy, and what such policy might consist of in reality. Further than that, it will aim to make the case for why policy for play should be among the priorities for government whatever the prevailing economic climate, or political party in power.

Arguably, the first major breakthrough in UK play policy happened in the English capital. Therefore, we will look at how the London Plan (Mayor of London, 2004b), the spatial development strategy for one of the world's biggest cities, included a policy that paved the way for individual play strategies for each of the 33 London Boroughs (Mayor of London, 2005), as well as supplementary planning guidance (Mayor of London, 2008) that established authoritative minimum standards for play space in new developments. We will consider how this initiative in London created a template for local government planning for play (Voce, 2006) that was adopted by the UK's biggest non-statutory funder, the Big Lottery Fund, as it made the production of play strategies by each of England's 355 local councils a key to probably the world's largest ever public funding programme for children's play. In particular, we will look at how these developments culminated in the Play Strategy, (DCSF/DCMS, 2008b), the unprecedentedly ambitious, wide-ranging and long-term national government plan for children's play in England, produced just as the financial crisis was unfolding.

The austerity measures that the UK government took in response to the crash of 2007–8 have cast a long shadow over many aspects of social policy in the years since, but play policy – especially in England, where there is no devolved national administration – has been especially badly affected. The Play Strategy was one of the first casualties of the coalition's policy cull, which began soon after it took office in the summer of 2010 (HM Treasury, 2010a, 2010b). The withdrawal of funding from local play provision in the intervening years has been widespread (Children's Rights Alliance for England, 2014). Finally, the book will look at the future prospects for play policy in the light of the unexpected Conservative Party victory in the 2015 general election.

I hope the book will demonstrate that the UK government in 2000–8 did not so much make policy for play as adopt it incrementally through a complex relationship with independent, largely voluntary sector advocates, whereby it resisted the movement's key demands at the same time as providing just enough resources to undertake the work to make them more credible and more deliverable. In this regard, I hope that it is a good case study of democracy in action: a pluralistic society using discreet, relatively small amounts of taxpayers' money to allow a dedicated sector to explore and test the evidence for, and viability of a larger investment in, a social policy initiative for the common good; a challenge, therefore, to Oliver Letwin's assumption.

With notable exceptions, some of which feature in our story, most politicians would have remained in ignorance of children's right to play without their engagement by this sector: the organised play movement. The book aims, therefore, not just to consider how governments can meet their obligations to develop and implement play policy, but also how advocates can persuade them to do so: what 'insisting on it' might mean in practice.

One of the great pioneers of play provision in the UK was the landscape architect, Lady Marjorie Allen of Hurtwood. Most renowned for inspiring the adventure playground movement, which, in turn, gave birth to playwork, she was nevertheless a firm believer that defined and bespoke areas where not, on their own, the answer to urban children's deep need for space to play. On the contrary she (1968) exhorts local authorities to employ play specialists to work strategically: surveying their regions; auditing space and provision for play; working across departmental responsibilities in 'housing, education, parks and (public) health' to create liveable, playable streets and estates. She pleads, especially to planners, to 'bring more sensitive awareness into places where people live and where they bring up families [...] so that children and their parents can feel they belong to a community that is intimate[...]'.

The play policy developments of the noughties were 40 years and more in the making, but it is true that in the aftermath of the financial crisis and the subsequent change of government in 2010 it seemed that the progress represented by the Play Strategy, and the benefits that it had started to bring for children and communities, had been lost. The main purpose of this book, far from harking back to a golden era of opportunities now wasted, is to offer a template for all those who believe it is important that they are not.

Although the coalition government abandoned the Play Strategy in 2010, by the time of the general election of 2015 there were signs of a rekindling of interest. In 2014, the Cabinet Office asked the longstanding Children's Play Policy Forum for new evidence of the benefits of specific forms of play provision (Gill, 2014). Later the same year an All Party Parliamentary Group on Children's Health

(APPG, 2014) called for a similarly wide range of measures to those that had been planned under Labour's Play Strategy, but this time including a new statutory play duty on local authorities, similar to that introduced in Wales.

The final chapter of the book is therefore dedicated to setting out some recommendations: to offer a framework for government policy on play and a roadmap for its proponents. I hope these might be helpful to policymakers and advocates alike, helping to realise the UN's exhortation that children's right to play – far from being again forgotten – must now more than ever be integral to our shared vision for a more child-friendly and playable public realm, as part of a fairer society and a better world.

ONE

'To play and to dream'

Restoring play to the heart of the campaign for children's rights

Of all the human rights specific to children as defined by the UN Convention on the Rights of the Child (1989), the right to play has become known as 'the forgotten right'.[1] The UK, in this respect, is not untypical; although it has a reputation internationally for its progressive thinking on play (Hart, p xvii, this volume), only in Wales is there a clear statutory duty[2] on local authorities to make universal provision for it. And it is not only governments that seem to neglect the importance of play relative to other children's rights; in particular, the dominance of education over play provision as a recognised issue tends to be reflected in the work of children's rights' advocacy bodies too.

The Children's Rights Alliance for England (CRAE), for example, in its annual review of government action on the CRC, found that 'a child's right to play and recreation suffers from poor recognition of its importance, and a lack of investment by government at national and local level' (CRAE, 2014). The

---

[1] This does not imply that other rights contained in the CRC are necessarily more fully realised than the right to play; simply that the latter is more commonly neglected or dismissed by policymakers and adult society in general.

[2] The Education Act (1996), amended by the Education and Inspections Act (2006), specifies that local authorities shall ensure that 'facilities for primary and secondary education provide adequate facilities for recreation and social and physical training for children who have not attained the age of 13', but this is generally interpreted as a requirement for extra-curricular activities to be offered by schools and the Education Department, rather than as a wider duty.

review refers to the UNCRC's own report of 2008, which called on the UK government to guarantee Article 31 for all children. The review also found that, across the 32 (of 152) local authorities able to comply with a Freedom of Information request[3] on play budgets, there had been an 'overall reduction' of 54% between the years 2008-9 and 2014-15; despite this, in its subsequent recommendations the CRAE report calls for subsidies and quality benchmarks in early years settings and a statutory universal youth offer but has no proposals for play policy[4] (CRAE, 2014)

However, while the right to play may have been largely overlooked not only by the parties of government but also by those who would influence them on behalf of children, it was in fact a central part of the argument of the modern children's rights movement[5] at its origins early in the last century. The UN's General Comment No. 17 (2013) notes that an earlier Declaration of the Rights of the Child (UN, 1959) proclaimed that: 'society and the public authorities shall endeavour to promote the enjoyment of this right [to play]'. In fact, it was in 1913 that the right to play was at the forefront of the changes demanded by the embryonic movement that would lead all the way to the CRC.

It was in that year before the outbreak of the global conflicts that would define the century, that a short pamphlet was produced in the United States with the intriguing title: 'The Declaration of Dependence by the Children of America in Mines and Factories and Workshops Assembled' (McKelway, 1913). This began:

> Whereas, we are declared to have been born free and equal, and whereas, we are yet in bondage in this land of the free [...] be it resolved, that childhood is endowed with certain inherent and inalienable rights, among

---

[3] The Freedom of Information Act (2000) creates a public 'right of access' to information held by public authorities.

[4] CRAE rectified this in 2015, when its report that year echoed the recommendation of an All Party Parliamentary Group for a play provision to become a statutory duty.

[5] Collective action by adult society to protect and safeguard children's wellbeing is far from being a phenomenon of the modern world. The term 'modern children's rights movement' refers here to the combined international efforts in the last century that culminated in the CRC, and has since worked for its adoption and implementation by governments.

which are freedom from toil for daily bread; the right
to play and to dream [...]

It is tempting to imagine here the collective mind of young
America playfully at work, subversively parodying the country's
most hallowed text (Jefferson et al, 1776). Linguistically flamboyant
as it was, this was a nonetheless solemn declaration of American
children's right to a protected childhood, in defiance of the
increasingly extensive and unforgiving use of child labour by the
burgeoning economy. The statement was designed to shame a
country that valued freedom above all else out of a collective denial
that it was effectively enslaving its poorest and most vulnerable in
service to a rapidly expanding and rapacious manufacturing base:
one of the worst 'evils incidental to incipient industrialism' (Adler,
1908).

The document was not, of course, drafted by labouring children,
but drawn up and published on their behalf by the National Child
Labour Committee (NCLC), a focal point for the movement to
constrain and ultimately abolish the practice. The NCLC's successful
campaign led over time to the broader movement for children's
rights worldwide and, from this perspective, the 'Declaration of
Dependence' can be seen as one of the earliest antecedents to the
CRC.

Leaving aside the irony that the United States remains possibly
the only country in the world to have not ratified the CRC,[6] what
is most striking about the 1913 declaration from the perspective of
the children's rights movement today is its assertion that childhood
should be protected as a phase of life free from the responsibilities
of the adult world. Its satirical invocation of the United States
Declaration of Independence asserts that children's rights are as
inviolable as those of their parents, but that their vulnerability and
natural dependency confers a particular duty on society to safeguard
them from the often harsh demands of economic survival. Its
impassioned plea against industrial exploitation defines childhood
as a time not to work, but 'to play and to dream'.

---

[6] In January 2015, IPA reported that the South Sudanese President had signed the
CRC but was awaiting official confirmation of its ratification. This would leave the
US as the only country in the world to have not ratified the treaty (IPA, 2015).

Via the 1959 declaration and an earlier one by the UN's predecessor, the League of Nations (1924), the CRC was agreed in 1989 by the overwhelming majority of the world's governments as the first legally binding international instrument to recognise and protect human rights specifically for children. It established the overarching framework for advocacy and action for children's rights: a powerful tool for the movement and a means by which to measure and monitor progress towards its implementation by government.

The main thrust of the children's rights movement globally has been to combat poverty, abuse and exploitation of children on the one hand; and to promote their education, health and wellbeing on the other (Robinson, 2005). In the minority world, certainly in the UK, it has also often been characterised by an emphasis on children's participation. This is covered by Article 12 of the Convention: children's right to be heard, generally interpreted as young people's engagement with decision-making processes that often seem to ape the models and protocols of the adult world of work and assume an agency in children that can effectively express itself in such fora.

Such activity often seems to model itself on the political activism and democratic participation of adult society. So children and young people are invited and supported to form councils and committees, or to take seats on those of adults. Services 'designed around the child' include vulnerable young people in a succession of chaired meetings between the professionals who have some duty to discharge in relation to them.

The statutory Office of the Children's Rights Commissioner for England, which has produced studies and sought reform on issues as diverse as teenage gang violence and food additives, also places a premium on including children in the organisational processes and structures by which it functions. Young people are involved at many levels of the office's business, such as conducting interviews for new staff and sitting on the many committees and forums that steer the Commissioner's work. Every year the Commissioner's office organises a 'Takeover Challenge' to promote children's rights. The concept is that organisations 'open their doors to children and young people to take over adult roles. It puts children and young people into decision-making positions and encourages organisations and businesses to hear their views' (Children's Commissioner, 2015).

Given a glimpse of this aspect of the movement that began by campaigning to end their premature enrolment into the world of work, the 'Children of America in Mines, Factories and Workshops Assembled' in 1913 may have been puzzled that an annual event designed to highlight the importance of children's rights in a later age, did so by sending them to do adult jobs for a day. Our introduction explored how the nature of children's play tends to cause it to be overlooked, but there is an argument that some of the priorities and methods of the children's rights movement, in sometimes equating children's participatory rights with the civil rights of minority groups, is at least partly responsible for this. The models for promoting and advocating for children's rights must arguably adopt the forms of political engagement and strategies for institutional change that are effective elsewhere, but making the inclusion of children themselves in that milieu almost a prerequisite of such activism's legitimacy has perhaps inadvertently served to also relegate the importance of play within the movement.

This is perhaps an inevitable consequence of the increasingly 'dominant discourse' to inform and underpin child policy, conceiving childhood as primarily a time of preparation for adulthood, and children's play therefore as the medium for acquiring and practising the skills for later life. Sutton-Smith (1997) may have said 'the opposite of play [...] is not work', but it is also true that the way in which most institutions work leaves little room for play. The 'play ethic' (Kane, 2004) has not yet replaced the work ethic and, while many young people undoubtedly learn much from participation activity – not just about the world of work but also about the politics and processes of democratic engagement – at its worst it can resemble nothing so much as facilitated work experience. Although there are no doubt many exceptions, younger children and those less articulate or self-confident tend not to be included. They, their play and its significance are overlooked.

McKelway and colleagues' challenge to the good society of the early 'American Century' (Evans, 1998) drew on a deeper, more resonant concept; one that emerged strongly in the Romantic movement and took hold in Victorian society. This was the idea of a 'good childhood'. Cunningham (2007) identifies the Romantics' depiction of children at play as being both central to community life and civilised humanity's closest connection to the purity and harmony of nature. The poems of Blake and Wordsworth eulogise childhood as the time when we are most fully alive; a sacred, almost mythical phase of life, the honouring of which keeps adult society closer connected to what is most important. Children's play is central to this vision, as Blake (1789) illustrates:

> When the voices of children are heard on the green
> And laughing is heard on the hill,
> My heart is at rest within my breast
> And everything else is still...
> 'Well, well, go and play till the light fades away
> And then go home to bed.'
> The little ones leaped and shouted and laugh'd
> And all the hills echoed. (Blake, 1789)

This vision of children – in touch with their vitality, happily playing in nature but also securely sheltered within the pastoral idylls that were the villages and hamlets of a 'green and pleasant land' (Blake, 1808) – is, of course, an idealisation, not only of childhood but also of traditional rural life. Nevertheless, it is one that resonated deeply with the mores and yearnings of the industrial society that was leaving many such scenes behind. It is not simply the children who are fulfilled in this playful arcadia, but also the nurse of the title, who, in finding such peace in the sounds of playing children, speaks for the universal parent-carer. What were people working for, if not to provide this for their children?

While the reality of most children's lives has often been harsher and always more complex, this romantic ideal of childhood with play at its heart endures. It may now be overlaid with widespread, often misplaced anxiety for their safety (Furedi, 2002), but while the majority of the population no longer lives in the countryside, the deep desire for our children to have the space and the freedom to play – happy, care-free and fulfilled – is a shared aspiration at least as strong as our wish for a secure future for them (Play England/ICM, 2009).

Instrumental in the UN's decision to issue GC17 was the publication of a working paper (Lester and Russell, 2010) for the International Play Association (IPA), which set out evidence to suggest that children's play is far more central and significant to an holistic approach to children's rights than its generally lowly status in child policy would seem to imply. In Lester and Russell's analysis there is an 'inherent tension in the CRC between children's right to express their views, and the principle of acting in the child's best interests'. Rather than seeking to resolve this tension by making Article 12 the touchstone of the movement, they suggest that more attention should be given to the 'primary form of participation [...] interwoven into everyday life' that is children's play.

In fact, say Lester and Russell (2010), play is essential and integral to each of the four principles of the CRC: non-discrimination, survival and development, the best interests of the child and participation. By ensuring the 'social and physical environment can support children's ability to play', society, they argue, will also be promoting their protection far more effectively than any amount of risk assessment or health and safety training. Playing cultivates the 'self-protecting process that offers the possibility to enhance adaptive capabilities and resilience'. They conclude that, contrary to its more common treatment by public policy, 'play is not a luxury to be considered after other rights'.

Lester and Russell (2008a), echoing Sutton-Smith (1997), challenge the dominant discourse by suggesting that the real benefits of playing – from a trans-disciplinary perspective that takes in neuroscience and anthropology as well as evolutionary biology and psychology – may be much more immediate, with play being its own reward. They do not say that play is not important to children's development (they are in good company in finding that it is key), but that children's own, intersubjective agency in their play is paramount. For children, being in control, encountering both the freedom and the responsibility that this implies, feeling uncertain and exercising choice are fundamental elements of playing that are undermined by the intervention of adults with instrumental agendas, however benign.

The theme of children's agency also features in the work of Moss and Petrie (2002), who have developed a critique of mainstream children's services, especially childcare, suggesting that the underlying assumptions and theories of policy and practice in this area conspire – consciously or not – to effectively oppress children rather than empower them. They argue that professional and institutional perspectives on children tend to see them as 'poor and weak': the 'passive dependants' on, and 'private responsibility' of, their parents.

They put forward a different proposition, but rather than theorising about what kind of services – or spaces – such an alternative discourse might lead to in terms of policy, practice and design, they describe a real working alternative. In contrast to the more common kind of 'primarily technical and disciplinary undertakings' of most schools, which they characterise as bringing to mind 'factories processing children on behalf of adults, in order to produce 'better adults for the future', their example is a space for children that, instead, empowers them 'in the here and now'. Their study of this alternative type of provision finds that in the course of using it, 'children gradually come to take responsibility for it', from undertaking routine maintenance to designing and building its structures and interviewing new staff. The latter do not direct or instruct children, but support, explain and negotiate. There is no authoritarian regime or required curriculum. '[C]hildren have the expectation that staff will respect them.' As one worker describes, 'staff respect children for what they are, not for what they want them to become.' The model described by Petrie and Moss is not an alternative school, but an adventure playground – the Venture, in Wrexham, North Wales – and it was from the loose network of adventure playground practitioners and advocates that there emerged, over the last four decades of the twentieth century, an increasingly cohesive and effective UK play movement: one that would eventually lead to wide-ranging and ambitious government policies for play.

TWO

'For a change'

Finding the evidence for play policy

Play practitioners and advocates tend to resist the imposition of extraneous agendas onto the play environment. It is one of the playwork principals (PPSG, 2005). But in the policy world of quantifiable outcomes, measurable impacts, cost–benefit ratios and the like, this can be a problem. Politicians – and perhaps electors too – want policy to be demonstrably effective. If public money or legislative authority is to be invested in something, then it had better produce results. Playing does not produce results; at least, not predictable ones of the kind that can easily be measured, evaluated and reported on.

Playing is an instinctive and universal human behaviour. In its way, it is as simple and as complex as anything else in nature. It is self-evident when children are playing, yet difficult to pin down where it starts and where it finishes (Sutton-Smith, 1997). This paradoxical quality – of something natural and innate on the one hand, yet complex and indefinable on the other – is further complicated for play advocates by the inconvenient truth that the more we learn about it, the clearer it becomes that play's primary purpose is simply to enjoy and become better at playing. Children play because it is in their nature, but it serves no subjective purpose other than to be enjoyed and to enhance itself.

Of course, we know in general terms that children's play does enhance their prospects. We can say that children who are allowed a good amount of time to play in the right environments will tend to be healthier, develop faster and do better in school than those who are not (Lester and Russell, 2008); but the specific benefits, and the risks too, are unpredictable.

But even accepting the important role of play in children's development, any approach that seeks to capture and measure the impact of different variables is going to quickly come up against the dilemma of how to monitor it without manipulating it. Theorists and practitioners alike – and not only those advocating the playwork approach – have argued that even introducing the concept of measurable outcomes to children's play risks perverting a complex, ancient and delicate dynamic, interfering with the child's experience and undermining a profound biological process (House, ed, 2011).

There are practical as well as ethical dimensions to the reluctance to monitor and evaluate play. The curtailed national evaluation of the Play Strategy (Frearson et al, 2013) noted that 'research on play outcomes is inherently difficult because of the contextual, elusive and fluid nature of play'. Experienced playworkers know that one of the anomalies of their role is that many of the richest play experiences happen out of the reach of adult eyes and ears. We all know, or suspect, that children behave differently when we are not around. This is why dens, hidey holes and other 'secret' places have such a sacred place in the playwork cannon, and why playworkers know not to cross those thresholds without good cause.

Notwithstanding these reservations, the pursuit of resources to research and develop credible evidence about play and play provision has been a major objective of the play movement, in particular since the Secretary of State for Culture, Chris Smith (see page 65), exhorted us in 1998 to rise to just this challenge. He had seen how important it was that the sector should find a way to reconcile its misgivings about 'measurable outcomes' for play, with the need to find an evidence base that could demonstrate the value of investing public money in provision for it.

There is not sufficient space here – and neither is the author qualified – to take more than a brief and selective stroll through what is a highly diverse range of perspectives and studies relevant to the question of how society might best respond to children's need to play. For our purposes a brief summary will suffice (and the bibliography contains many rich sources for further exploration).

It would be conventional at this point to define, or at least say what we mean by 'play'. Policy makers, not unreasonably, like to define what it is they are making policy for, and academics, for different reasons, also need to be exact. Settling on a definition of play is, however, somewhat problematic, for two contrasting reasons. First, beginning a treatise on something as commonplace as children's play by attempting to answer the question 'what is it?' risks patronising the reader. Anyone who has ever spent time with children, or can remember being one, knows what play is and what playing feels like. The word is not a piece of jargon that needs explaining to the uninitiated. Second, and paradoxically, play is such an elemental, ubiquitous phenomenon – manifesting so many traits, engaging so many facets of our species – that any attempt to pin it down to a few words or sentences will inevitably either fall short or miss an essential point. It is also, within a serious analysis, famously 'ambiguous' (the other side of the coin to its ubiquity); to such a degree, in fact, that Sutton-Smith (1997) dedicated one of his most celebrated works to its very indefinability, warning at the outset that 'when it comes to making theoretical statements about what play is, we fall into silliness'.

The plain-speaking Labour MP Frank Dobson ignored this caution – he was not in the business of making theoretical statements – and adopted, for the purposes of his Play Review (DCMS, 2003), the simple statement that play is 'what children and young people do when they follow their own ideas, in their own way and for their own reasons'. This was effectively a 'plain English' adaptation of the playwork definition, which speaks of play as 'a process that is freely chosen, personally directed and intrinsically motivated' PPSG, 2005). The Dobson version became the standard definition of play for the policy initiatives in England that followed, although the research literature suggests, as Sutton-Smith warned, that it is not so simple.

Different perspectives on play

Several different scientific and academic disciplines take a keen interest in the phenomena of play and playing. Unsurprisingly, they each have different things to say about it: most if not all of them complementary. Biology and evolutionary sciences like epigenetics[1]

---

[1] Epigenetics is the study of changes in organisms caused by modification of gene expression (heritable traits) by influences other than alteration of the genetic code, such as adaptation to the environment.

consider the nature and role of play in the lives of the young in terms of how they develop and mature, and in the ethology[2] of species as a whole in terms of how they adapt and evolve. Brown and Patte (2013) identifies three strands to the evolutionary theories of play. The first is the surplus energy theory of Schiller ([1794] 2012) and Spencer (1864), whereby the animal species best equipped to survive and thrive do so partly by expending excess energy through play, thereby maintaining the physical capability to rise to adaptive challenges: 'survival of the fittest' (Spencer, 1864).

Modern studies (Mackett and Paskins, 2008) of the calorific efficiency of children at play (not to mention the experience of anyone who has watched them for any length of time!) confirm that playing 'in fields of free action' (Lester and Russell, 2008) frequently involves intense levels of physical activity, even compared to rigorous organised sports. Unlike sports, however, the activity is spontaneous, expressive of playful instincts and for no reward except enjoyment. Thus children rest and exert their bodies alternately in a self-regulated, natural rhythm over sustained periods. So convinced was he of the physical benefits of free play that Dietz (2001), warning of the coming epidemic of obesity in British children, opined that the 'main solution' was 'to simply turn off the TV and let them play'.

The second evolutionary theory of play cited by Brown and Patte was developed by Karl Groos (1901).Developing the theories of Schiller and Spencer, Groos views playing as the means by which the young of species, more than burning off energy, are learning the adaptive skills to survive. Thus play fighting and locomotive play, for example, see children rehearsing – in the safety of the play frame – their responses to the challenges and dangers they will face, and developing the skills to meet them. Finally, Brown and Patte (2013) identify a less intuitive theory developed in the field of evolutionary psychology by Baldwin (1896), which sees the play of children as the means by which we express primitive inherited instincts from our ancestral past so as not to be constrained or inhibited by them as we face new adaptive challenges.

The psychologies of various schools, not just evolutionary but also developmental and psychoanalytic, each situate children's play

---

[2] Ethology is the science of animal, including human, behaviour and social organisation from a biological perspective.

as central to the individual's formation of his or her sense of self and the capacity to relate; but whereas developmental psychology (for example Piaget, 1951; Vygotsky, 1967) has focused on its role as a catalyst for mental processes – the capacity to think, calculate and analyse – other areas, such as deep psychology (for example Jung, 1944; Klein, 1975) have equally explored the importance of play to emotional development and regulation, transpersonal awareness and connectedness.

Evolutionary psychology and psychoanalytic theory each conceive play to be the chief medium for the child's developing sense of self, his or her ability to distinguish self from 'other', and to enjoin the 'potential space' for relationship (Winnicott, 1964). Thus the earliest bonding between an infant and its mother is through playful sounds and gestures. Fagen (2011) notes that although play behaviours are clearly an important part of the evolutionary story of many animal species, in comparison to our nearest relatives, the great apes, 'human infants aged 2-6 months are still at a uniquely early stage of development'. The necessary holding, eye contact and intimate communication may mean that 'infant–mother social contingency play arguably has unique roles in human development' wherein the uniquely extended dependence of the human baby confers a particular role on 'the mother (or other adult) in framing, shaping, and modulating' its play in order 'to allow play itself to develop so that it can emerge, ready to function' as the child matures. Fagen (2011) refers to this uniquely human phase of early infancy (two to six months) as a 'primary developmental project' in which 'something extraordinary is needed to produce the necessary result'. No one who has ever played with an infant would argue.

Where that extraordinary process is disturbed, it is play (of course) that provides the child with its own adaptive life rafts, providing ways to reconcile herself to traumatic events (Winnicott, 1971). 'Transitional objects' (such as a precious cuddly toy or 'security blanket') are deeply entwined with the child's earliest play moments and can be the subject of transferred 'attachment' (Bowlby, 1969; Ainsworth, 1973), enabling children to retain a degree of control and a sense of safety in the face of distressful circumstances such as abandonment, trauma or loss. Brown (2015) tells movingly of a young girl, bereaved of her mother, playing constantly and with great care with a particular doll whom she names 'Mum'.

It is important to note, though, that to the extent that there are important therapeutic benefits to playing – and play therapy is an established branch of clinical psychology – it is also seen as being of vital importance to the wellbeing of emotionally healthy children and fulfilled, self-aware adults: 'It is in playing and only in playing that the individual child or adult is able to be creative and to use the whole personality, and it is only in being creative that the individual discovers the self' (Winnicott, 1971).

As the terms suggest, evolutionary psychology extends the Darwinian theory of natural selection to suggest that psychological (mental, emotional, interpersonal) traits, just like physical ones, are formed by a process of adaptation – over generations – to environmental factors, and that the play of the young of species, both in cementing bonds with their adult care givers and in the 'wild play' (Hughes, 2001) that this primary attachment provides them with the security to express – environment permitting – is a key process by which such adaptation occurs and is passed on (Burghardt, 2005).

One of the fastest developing areas of medical research is in neuroscience, where advances in technology have enabled increasingly sophisticated brain mapping and the analysis that this affords. Play – or more particularly, the mental and emotional activity triggered through play – has been found through these methods to be an important stimulant of the synaptogenesis (that is, the formation of new connections between brain cells, or synapses) that is most prolific in early childhood. From this perspective, playing literally helps the brain – the whole nervous system, in fact – to construct itself and its relationship with the rest of the body-mind. The motivation and reward centres of the brain are especially significant in this process.

Sociological and anthropological perspectives on play highlight its central place, albeit differently in different societies, within the culture of childhood. Children's geographies, peer alignments and traditional forms of child-initiated expression are manifested through playing together as part of communities. Play is also identified as a means of understanding – or at least apprehending – adult culture and societal norms, but then often adapting or subverting them to serve children's different purposes (primarily to have fun with them).

What each of the scientific perspectives tend to suggest is that play, like childhood itself, is 'complex and emergent, and because this is so, its understanding requires a broad set of intellectual resources, an interdisciplinary approach and an open-minded process of inquiry' (Prout, 2005).

Lester and Russell (2008) of the University of Gloucestershire took just such an approach when Play England commissioned them to undertake a play research review in 2006. Much had been done within this fast developing, multi-disciplinary field since the work (Cole-Hamilton, Harrop and Street, 2002) that underpinned CPC's *Making the case for play* report (Cole-Hamilton and Gill, 2002), which first called for a national play strategy. The aim now was to produce an up-to-date appraisal not only of the different perspectives afforded by the science of play but also of how these informed policy and practice – or not.

Lester and Russell's (2008) transdisciplinary approach to the study of play identified certain universal processes that bind play, development and wellbeing together in a relationship that has much bearing on the nature of resilience. These are highlighted below:

The Benefits of Play

- **Emotion regulation:** play enhances the development of flexible and adaptive emotions.
- **Pleasure and enjoyment and the promotion of positive feelings:** play, as an enjoyable experience, promotes positive affect, which in turn encourages further exploration, novelty and creativity.
- **Stress response systems:** play offers the opportunity to create and resolve uncertainty (Spinka et al, 2001; Sutton-Smith, 2003).
- **Creativity:** the key relationship between play and creativity exists in the flexibility of responses to novel and uncertain situations and the non-serious interpretation of a range of stimuli.
- **Learning:** the primary benefits of play are found within the integration of motivation, emotion and reward systems rather than the higher cognitive aspects of brain development (Burghardt, 2005).

- **Attachment:** play has a central role, from the first moments of life through to adulthood, in developing strong attachments.
- **Place attachment:** just as children need strong social attachments, attachment to place may also be seen as a key adaptive system. The creation of a sense of place is vital not only to a sense of wellbeing but also to maintaining the quality and vitality of the environment. (Lester and Russell, 2008)

In their critical analysis of how policy has applied this knowledge in practice, Lester and Russell (2008) found that the dominant discourse in the contemporary era had tended to take its premise from only one of the several possible perspectives – developmental psychology. Citing Smith (2005), they found that 'children's play has been "co-opted" in modern, industrialised societies as a way of improving cognitive and social skills': what Sutton-Smith (1998) calls the 'progress rhetoric', which is more a result of political and cultural hegemony than of an objective reading of a fuller range of evidence. Their main thesis was that because the benefits of playing were more immediate than deferred, and the main learning from play was simply how to play more and better, it was erroneous to conceive of children's play as primarily instrumental to their accelerated learning, improved health or other 'outcomes' and that to do so was to misunderstand the nature of play, leading to erroneously conceived and designed responses to it in policy and practice from public services and public space.

These conclusions were a challenge to a government elected on the slogan 'education, education, education' that wanted to drive up academic attainment by all means possible, including a template for 'extended services', childcare and even holiday play schemes that conceived all such services as opportunities mainly for learning. Paradoxically, however, the overarching framework for New Labour's reform agenda for children's services, Every Child Matters, was one crying out for a more holistic approach to the research-policy-practice triad and just such a transdisciplinary perspective of the evidence and science informing it. For services (including schools, albeit reluctantly) to work to improve 'universal outcomes' for all children, they would need, clearly, to respond to a fuller appreciation of children's needs, aspirations and motivations than simply how they best acquire skills, retain information, follow rules and take instruction. Furthermore, although Lester and Russell (2008) asserted that 'if policy-makers accept the evidence for the significance of play for children's well-being and development, then play provision should be judged on whether it enables children to play rather than on more instrumental outcomes', they also concluded – and this was the 'policy fit' contained in what was an otherwise radical report from the perspective of established doctrine – that although 'there is no guarantee that playing will deliver on the five Every Child Matters outcomes; we can, however, be confident that these outcomes are more likely to be realised if children can play'.

However equivocal, making this link within such a scholarly and critical analysis was vitally important to those of us seeking to convince ministers that investing in children's play provision and exploring more play-friendly planning was both a good use of public funds and consistent with their overall approach.

Although *Play for Change* became a key document in the pursuit of government play policy, it was, paradoxically, frank in its assessment that there was little evidence of how best to manifest it. While Lester and Russell (2008) made the general observation from their study that public policy needed to cultivate an 'appreciation of the relationship between the nature of play and an environmental field of free action', suggesting that this 'is crucial in designing play friendly neighbourhoods,' they also had to acknowledge the dearth of evidence of what constitutes good play provision itself: the specific types of environment, services or spaces that policy should aim to create or support.

This was a natural consequence, they argued, of their main thesis: that the 'utilitarian' concept of play within established policy meant that 'much of the literature on practice aims to show instrumental outcomes for play provision – there is a need to gather the evidence on what works best in providing for play for its own sake'. In the meantime, there was playwork theory and practice to draw on. Here, the work of Bob Hughes and its adoption by CPC and their allies in Best Play (Children's Play Council et al, 2000) was critical.

A practitioner and researcher in his own right, Hughes was a keen student of the literature on play who applied his understanding of the evolutionary and brain sciences to a lifelong study of children on adventure playgrounds, essentially defining the theory and practice of playwork in the process. Hughes's seminal Evolutionary Playwork (2001) included his analysis of 'criteria for an enriched play environment', which he also contributed to Best Play, with examples against each criterion:

- A varied and interesting physical environment;
- Challenge in relation to the physical environment;
- Activities which test the limits of capabilities;
- Playing with the natural elements: earth, water, fire, air;
- Movement, such as running, jumping, rolling, climbing, balancing;
- Manipulating natural and fabricated materials;
- Stimulation of the five senses;
- Experiencing change in the natural and built environment;
- Social interactions;
- Playing with identity;
- Experiencing a range of emotions.

By the 2000s, children not able to access one of the country's network[3] of adventure playgrounds, which (to a greater or lesser extent) aimed to offer each of these opportunities to children, were not quite prisoners in their own homes; but there is no question that the constraints on children's 'freedom to roam' – to play outside, unsupervised – had dramatically decreased since the 1970s. A study on road safety for the Policy Studies Institute (Hillman et al, 1990) found that between 1971 and 1990, the proportion of seven- and eight-year-old children allowed to go to school without adult supervision – a good proxy indicator of children's freedom to play outside – fell from 80% in 1971 to a mere 9% by 1990. The growing ubiquity of TV, computers, game consoles and other electronic amusements – whatever their intrinsic benefits – was happily filling the gap in children's play lives, leading to a generation of children with such sedentary lifestyles that childhood obesity was soon to reach epidemic levels (Dietz, 2001).

---

[3]   A project by PLAYLINK in 1999–2000 estimated that there were 250–75 adventure playgrounds in the UK, depending on how they were defined. The number is now undoubtedly considerably lower.

Webb and Brown (2003), Hughes (2003) and Gill (2007) have each highlighted the wider consequences of 'play deprivation' for children's current wellbeing and future health and development. And although there is a weight of evidence to prove that problems arise from constraints on children's play, demonstrating the corollary – the effectiveness, especially the cost-effectiveness, of specific types of play provision in combating such problems or engendering benefits – has been hard to come by. Most play projects are not set up to monitor and evaluate with the rigour required of empirical studies, and such activity is counterintuitive to playwork practice.

Nevertheless, an Economic Analysis of Play Provision (Matrix Evidence, 2010) commissioned by Play England estimated that 'every £1 invested in an adventure playground generates £1.32 in social benefits' over a 20-year period, and that over the same period 'the benefits generated by an adventure playground compared with no playground exceed the costs by £0.67 million'. The report concluded that cutting the funding for adventure playgrounds would therefore cost more than it would save.

More recently, the Children's Play Policy Forum, responding to a request from the Cabinet Office, has attempted to demonstrate the cost-effectiveness of play provision. It tasked Tim Gill to 'look at quantitative evidence of the wider outcomes and impact of play interventions and initiatives' (Gill, 2014) . Unsurprisingly he found evidence of the benefits of playwork services and a playable public realm to be 'patchy and fragmented', citing the 'comparative lack of studies and evaluations'. Leaving aside the irony that probably the most thorough pilot and evaluation of such interventions ever commissioned – the Play Pathfinder programme of 2008–11 – was scrapped by the same government now asking for such evidence, Gill's report illustrates the flaw in following the strictly evidence-based approach. While asserting that 'the improvement of opportunities for outdoor play can and should be seen as a valid, worthwhile outcome in its own right' (Gill, 2014) , the report qualifies this by admitting that 'there may be a need for more quantitative research on the detailed relationship between various benefits and children's experiences of play'. It concludes that the most convincing evidence is of the promotion of children's physical activity during school break times, where these support free play – with only 'modest evidence' (Gill, 2014) of other benefits and from other settings.

THREE

'Advocates for play'

Playwork's place at the heart of the play movement

Behind a high, black, wooden fence that all but entirely obscures it from view, an old Thames riverboat, now converted to serve as a unique indoor play space for local children, is the centrepiece of what appears to be an abandoned plot of waste ground, left over from a slum clearance in the 1950s or 1960s.

The fence was erected as a precondition for the award of a capital funding grant from an inner-city investment scheme in the 1980s; for this site – deemed unsightly to all but the local children, for whom it is simply 'the Barge' – occupies a high-profile position: opposite the famous Old Vic theatre in the Waterloo area of inner London, less than a mile from the Houses of Parliament and even closer to the South Bank arts complex. As if the rusting old boat were not enough, the winers, diners and theatregoers passing by were also subject to the sight of the sprawling, somewhat anarchic homemade wooden structures that children and their playworkers were prone to erecting without apparent consideration of the aesthetic sensibilities the cultural elite – hence the fence.

Today however, this slightly ramshackle place, which is in a process of seemingly endless redevelopment, is being visited, paradoxically, by someone at the pinnacle of this elite: no less than Her Royal Highness Princess Anne, only daughter of the reigning monarch. As a patron of the local charity Blackfriars Settlement, Princess Anne is to visit some of its projects on the occasion of its centenary. One of these is the Barge, otherwise known as Waterloo Adventure Playground.

Sniffer dogs and armed police sweep through the grounds in advance and one of the children has given me (as the senior playworker and site manager) an anxiety attack by claiming that there's 'a shooter' buried somewhere behind the barge. This is not entirely incredible, given the networks of some of the local families whose children attend the facility, including, for example, those of the notorious 'Great Train Robbers'. No gun is found, however. I can breathe again.

The Princess arrives, and while it is unlikely that a more incongruous scene has been observed in SE1 for many years, she is completely charming, relaxed and interested in the assorted children, staff and parents there to greet her, once she is freed from the accompanying cortège. Some of the children show her a scale model that they have built of how the playground will look once the latest round of rebuilding is complete. She is visibly impressed that these are not only their ideas, but that they will themselves be actively involved in their construction.

Noticing the fire pit, she encourages the children present to tell her about the marshmallow toasts and how they enjoy telling stories around the flames on the cooler evenings. She seems genuinely impressed when she hears about the freedom and control that children have here, and especially at the sense of community and social connection they exhibit: that this is their place, of which they are immensely proud.

Before she moves on to the next project, this most privileged of women, the Princess Royal, turns to me and says – evidently quite sincere – that these children, from the 'deprived' social housing estates in the looming shadow of Waterloo Station, seem be enjoying the kind of childhood that many supposedly better-off children would relish.

The 1960s, 1970s and 1980s were boom years for the grassroots community play provision embodied by adventure playgrounds like the Barge. Shaping and manipulating environments and deploying loose parts, large and small, is an important part of children's play whenever there is an opportunity for it (Nicholson, 1971). The waste grounds and decaying urban landscapes of post-war Britain offered an abundance of such adventures. Inner-city children, increasingly squeezed out of public space by planners, traffic and changing attitudes to them (Hurtwood, 1968) – and a long way from the bucolic idylls of Wordsworth and Blake – had taken to exploring and colonising old bombsites and demolished housing blocks, turning them into ad hoc play areas that offered better prospects than their increasingly crowded streets or non-existent gardens.

Danish architect Carl Theodor Sørensen is credited with coining the term 'junk playgrounds' in the 1930s to describe an approach to public playgrounds that responded to children's tendency to utilise found objects for their play (de Coninck-Smith, 1999). After some false starts John Bertleson developed the first site based on this idea in Emdrup, Copenhagen in 1943 (Cranwell, 2009a). In this site, seemingly ramshackle makeshift structures and dens, open fires, improvised homemade toys assembled from whatever scrap materials were available, and supportive adults on hand to help with bike repairs and the use of tools all offered a very different range of experiences to the fixed swings and roundabouts found in public parks.

British landscape architect and play space pioneer Lady Allen of Hurtwood is widely credited with bringing the concept to the UK and eventually calling them adventure playgrounds (Cranwell, 2009b). These home-made paradises for play developed their own unique architecture (Norman, 2004) of self-built wooden structures. Old telegraph poles, discarded scaffolding planks, worn tyres and donated shipping ropes were deployed to create mazes, platforms, runways and swings worthy of the name, all designed from the exuberance of children's own aspirations and allowing them to clamber, jump, wheel,[1] crawl, climb and swing to heights and over distances never dreamed of on the monkey bars and roundabouts of municipal playgrounds.

More adults got involved – sometimes from the social action traditions represented by Settlements such as the one in Blackfriars and Waterloo, but often forming their own small, independent

---

[1] Lady Allen was a pioneer not only of adventure playgrounds but also of play opportunities for disabled children, establishing the 'Handicapped Adventure Playground Association' (later part of Kids: www.kids.org.uk) dedicated to building playgrounds that put their needs first.

charities – helping kids to develop boundaries and rules, secure more resources, build indoor space for arts, crafts, cooking and music, and ultimately to establish the sites as more or less permanent fixtures. The playgrounds and their ethos developed and evolved. They became socially more inclusive so that younger children, girls, disabled children and children from minority ethnic communities could feel as much at home as the older white boys who, without playwork interventions, could sometimes tend to dominate. A wider range of activities became possible; sand, water and fire play were the norm, as was the use of scrap materials for everything from dress-up games to freeform art and sculpture (adventure playgrounds were the original 'upcyclers').

Many sites developed garden areas and kept animals. They held discos, entered football competitions and took children camping. Central to all of this, though, was always the child's choice. Children had an abundance of opportunities: to play with friends or alone, to build or dismantle, to play on structures or to mess about in fancy dress; but none of these were compulsory. This was their space, their time, to do exactly as they pleased. Adventure playgrounds became unique communities of children and adults, cooperating to create not only physical but also social and cultural environments, dedicated solely to children doing their own thing in their own way, even if this seemed to be nothing much at all (Brown, 2007).

Adventure playgrounds can be seen as a direct, practical response to the growing need of urban children to have their space to play protected and supported within the large-scale, high-rise housing developments – and the social changes that accompanied them – that swept through British cities after the postwar slum clearances. They were also to some degree part of a radical activism with links to the anarchist movement, which saw self-organisation and the reclaiming of land for social good as articles of faith in the face of the corporate commercial forces and patriarchal politics that were driving the new designs on the public realm (Ward, 1978).

In the way that adventure playgrounds (before being labelled as such or even much noticed by wider society) were first of all colonies of children making space to play for themselves within landscapes that did not overtly encourage it, they can be seen as a manifestation of our species' evolutionary instinct to survive: not in the fear-bound risk-averse sense but in the biological sense, in which the organism, as Lester and Russell (2010) observe, 'favourably position[s] itself [...] to maintain both current and future integrity and to respond to the demands of the environment'.

Whichever analysis (or combination of analyses) of the adventure playground movement one most accepts, it brought with it a generation of committed advocates for children's play who did not accept the 'education continuum' (Wilkin et al, 2003) – wherein all services for and spaces afforded to children are seen primarily as specific, adult-determined learning opportunities – as their paradigm. On adventure playgrounds, the 'dominant discourse' – as challenged in academia by Moss and Petrie (2002), Lester and Russell (2008) and others – was discarded in favour of an exciting new approach. A different way of working with children was being developed: one that placed supporting the child's play experience here and now at the centre of good practice and the creation of play spaces at the heart any wider social, cultural or physical space provided for them, regardless of 'measurable outcomes'. This was the emergence of playwork.

Playwork didn't just help children to build the playgrounds of their imaginations and to enjoy them as integral, essential parts of their childhood domain, compensating for the lack of natural play space afforded by their wider environment. It also served to radicalise successive generations of people working with children to an alternative vision of children's place in society and the appropriate adult response. Playwork assumes that 'the impulse to play is innate [...] a biological, psychological and social necessity [...] fundamental to the healthy development and wellbeing of individuals and communities' (PPSG, 2005). The Playwork Principles define the role of the playworker as being 'to support and facilitate the play process and this should inform the development of play policy, strategy, training and education' (PPSG, 2005). In a world where the structuring of time and resources around children's formal learning dominates their lives and 'education, education, education' is seen as an election-winning slogan, playwork practice recognises different priorities and positions its practitioners as advocates: not for the 'voice of the child' in the Article 12 sense of participatory democracy, but for their right to play and to dream. For playworkers, 'the play process takes precedence; playworkers are advocates for play when engaging with adult-led agendas' (PPSG, 2005). Their purpose is not to simply provide and support play opportunities within designated areas and at appointed times, but to champion play in all other areas and at all other times, campaigning for greater recognition and more resources for play 'to ensure […] that children's physical and social environments support their play', as called for by Lester and Russell (2010).

One of the barriers to promoting play policy that would include staffed provision is an instinctive aversion to the idea of adults intervening in what should be children's own time and space. Yet playworkers are often the fiercest defenders of the child's domain, resisting attempts by well-meaning but misguided institutions to harness and manipulate what should be uncontainable, spontaneous, even wild (Hughes, 2001). It is a first principle of playwork that children's play is 'personally directed and intrinsically motivated. That is, children and young people determine and control the content and intent of their play' (PPSG, 2005). A key tenet of good playwork practice might be described as 'low intervention-high response'. Playworkers aim to strike a balance between 'letting children have the freedom to play and discover things for themselves' and 'supporting [them] in their play by being responsive to their cues' (Stobart, 2001).

More than in any other supervised environment, children in a playwork setting will be allowed and supported to set their own agenda (or to have none), take their own decisions, manage their own risks and deal with the consequences. Uncertainty and unpredictability are watchwords in playwork, as practitioners seek to honour and serve the immediacy of the playing child. What price, then, the need to show how it helps to meet overarching policy objectives for health or learning, or to monitor such outcomes in objective quantifiable terms?

Playwork starts a long campaign

In the 1970s, when playwork was beginning to evolve from 'play-leadership' and to develop its campaigning muscles, a number of associations and alliances were formed. The Institute of Playleaders, the Association of Adventure Playworkers and Fair Play for Children were among the organisations that sprang up to provide vehicles for collective action to promote play provision and playwork (Cranwell, 2009a). The National Playing Fields Association had for many decades been a champion of children's play as part of its wider remit to protect and improve outdoor space for sport and games. As yet, however, there was no overall national body solely for children's play.

Holiday play schemes and after-school clubs also proliferated in the 1970s. Increasing numbers of women entering the workforce and other changes to family life gave rise to concerns about the phenomenon of 'latch-key kids': children letting themselves into the empty home when school was finished and their parents where still at work. In 1981, the association for after-school clubs – the National Out of School Alliance (NOOSA), later to become Kids Clubs Network and then 4Children – joined with some of these other organisations to lobby the government to provide funding for a national play organisation (Cranwell, 2009b). The following year Margaret Thatcher's Conservative government awarded funding – the first of its kind solely to support and promote children's play provision – to the Association for Children's Play and Recreation, which soon became known simply as Playboard.

This initial government contract was terminated after only three years and Playboard dissolved soon after, but the need for a national play body had become established (Cranwell, 2009b). In 1988, the government asked the Sports Council – an arms-length public body for the promotion of grassroots participation in sport – to take on responsibility for the growing non-commercial play sector. The Children's Play and Recreation Unit (CPRU) was established, which in turn issued contracts for a play information service to the National Playing Fields Association (NPFA); and for the development of recognised playwork training and qualifications to the national training organisation, Sprito.

The NPFA, founded by Royal Charter, had a long history as the country's leading play charity. It was at the Association's launch event in 1926 that the former Liberal Prime Minister and war leader David Lloyd George gave what has probably become the most quoted speech about children's play since Plato, encapsulating the entire argument for play policy in three memorable sentences: 'The right to play is the child's first claim in the community. Play is nature's training for life. No community can infringe that right without doing enduring harm to the minds and bodies of its citizens' (cited in Browne and Patte, 2013).

The NPFA had held the government contract for national information services – a highly valued play library and a bimonthly news journal, *Play Today* – since the demise of Playboard in 1986. While it was respected for its longevity, its expertise in planning and the legal protection of land for play, and its widely adopted six-acre standard (Torkildsen, 2012), the NPFA – with its traditionally conservative constituency of largely rural county playing fields' associations – was not the body to speak for adventure playgrounds with their urban character, or for playwork, with its radical edge.

Sprito was an industry body representing the sports, recreation and outdoor leisure sectors to government. Largely employer-led, it was another somewhat uncomfortable home for the play movement. With the demise of Playboard the different bodies that had lobbied for it regrouped, arguing that – notwithstanding the CPRU and the two government contracts – there was a need for an independent body to promote children's play and to freely campaign for more and better provision. The National Voluntary Council for Children's Play – later to become simply the Children's Play Council (CPC) – was born, and many of those around its table were former playworkers, schooled in the UK's adventure playgrounds.

By the 1990s, adventure playgrounds, having multiplied during the 1970s, were facing big challenges. The local authority grants that most of them relied on were minimal. Playworkers were poorly paid and often had little or no access to training. The former waste grounds that many playgrounds occupied, but which were still mostly owned by local authorities, had become prime real estate as towns and cities were redeveloped around them. Many were closed down as their councils cashed in or used the land for other priorities.

Another threat to the UK adventure playground movement – which had emerged organically from children's own initiative in seeking out the most playable places within the space afforded to them – ironically emerged from adult society's need to have children taken care of out of school. The growth of school-aged childcare, a key feature of successive governments' employment policies, saw many local authorities eyeing their local adventure playgrounds as prime candidates to meet the growing demand for registered places. The 'Childcare Revolution' had begun (Smith and Baker, 2000).

By the 1990s, although child labour in the UK was largely a thing of the past, children's daily lives were being demarcated on the one hand by an education system increasingly designed to meet the demands of the economy, and on the other by society's need to have them cared for while parents were at work. While the hardships may have been less draconian than those endured by children working in mines and factories of industrial Britain and the USA, modern children's right to play was hardly less constrained by the needs of adult society than it was in 1913.

Meanwhile, outside of school and childcare provision, traditional places in which to play – the streets, alleyways, woodland and open spaces in and around children's neighbourhoods – were becoming less and less accessible to them. Traffic; crime; fear of abuse or abduction; the 'atomisation' of residential communities (Wilby, 2007), the demonisation of children in public and the ubiquitous presence of electronic media were all being blamed for contributing to the modern phenomenon of the 'battery-reared child' (Gill, 2004). This was of course a caricature, but it was also a good metaphor for the realities of many primary school-aged children (see Chapter Two) and one that resonated with families, who, research suggested, knew that their children needed more time, space and permission to play but were often anxious to allow it (ICM Research, 2009).

Older children and teenagers, meanwhile, were coming under the ever more vigilant scrutiny of the law as moral panics about 'feral youth' gave rise to calls for greater policing of such 'anti-social behaviour' as playing football in the road, drawing hopscotch grids on the pavement (BBC News, 2013) or merely hanging out with friends in numbers that made polite society nervous. Children's right to play and to dream, which was for generations such an important affordance of the public realm, was now effectively returning to the status of idyllic – and now nostalgic – myth.

One outcome of the advocacy of McKelway and his colleagues in early 20th-century USA was the establishment of the United States Children's Bureau (Lindenmeyer, 1997), which exists to this day as a federal arm of the state dedicated to vulnerable children. It was perhaps fitting, then, that in the 1990s UK play advocates –

galvanised by the CRC (1989) and its recognition of the legal right to play, and seeking to coalesce and form new alliances to build the domestic case for action – found a home at Britain's own National Children's Bureau (NCB).

NCB at that time was a children's charity specialising in research and child policy development and providing office space and infrastructure support for a wide range of groups, alliances and councils working for different aspects of children's rights and wellbeing. The Council for Disabled Children, the Sex Education Forum and the Anti-Bullying Alliance are examples of the semi-independent bodies hosted, and to various degrees managed and administered, under the aegis of NCB. As CPC took stock of its options in the mid 1990s, gearing up for the campaigns ahead, it was NCB that offered a home.

In spite of the indifference of most politicians, CPC made a firm decision to base its campaigning and influencing activity on children's right to play, as recognised in Article 31 of the CRC. During the 1990s it organised its campaigning and advocacy work largely around a document that it produced in consultation with its members and allies, known as the Charter for Children's Play (CPC, 1998). Taking Article 31 as its starting point, the Charter set out ten principles, each aiming to expand on the child's right to play in different contexts, as follows:

1. **Children**

   All children need to play and have a right to play. Children of all ages should be able to play freely and confidently on their own and with other children.

2. **Parents and carers**

   Parents and other carers should respect and value their children's play and try and maximise their opportunities for safe and stimulating play within and outside the home.

3. **Play for all**

   All children should have equal access to play opportunities and services.

4. **Neighbourhood play**

   All our children should be able to play safely outdoors wherever they live, in cities and in the countryside. Older children should also be able to get around safely on their own.

5. **Play strategies**
   Central and local government and voluntary organisations should think creatively and strategically about children and their play.

6. **Play services**
   All children should have access to a range of good quality early years, play and out-of-school services such as play centres, holiday play schemes, adventure playgrounds, after-school clubs, playgrounds, toy libraries and play buses.

7. **Schools and play**
   All schools should support and facilitate children's play. Play and learning are not separate; play is part of learning and learning is part of play. Learning through play supports and enriches learning through formal education.

8. **Safe play**
   Play opportunities should challenge and stimulate children's abilities but not threaten their survival or wellbeing.

9. **Special play situations**
   Hospital admissions, visits to a doctor, or a stay in temporary accommodation are some of the situations where children are in strange surroundings, perhaps experiencing fear, pain, anxiety and discomfort.

10. **Playwork education and training**
    All playwork education and training should be flexible, adaptive and reflective of existing good practice in playwork and should involve a significant fieldwork practice component.

The Charter, which has been subsequently revised and republished by CPC's successor body, Play England (2006), has been criticised; some have pointed out that it is not strictly a Charter at all, and that its principles are in fact a rather vague set of aspirations for children's play. In its defence, CPC upheld that its purpose was to create a shared vision for play provision as part of the public realm and that its aims had to therefore be broad enough for interpretation and adoption by the various public authorities whose buy-in was essential to the mission.

In this regard the Charter can be said to have at least partially succeeded. Originally restricted to national voluntary organisations, in 1997 CPC extended its membership to include local authorities and regional charities, but only on the condition that they formally adopt the Charter at the level of their governing body. In the case of a local authority, this meant the council of elected members itself. Thus, those local authorities becoming members of CPC – giving them access to information, conferences, library services and so on, as well as a seat on the Council – went through a process of debating the issues contained in the Charter before formally adopting it. It was a campaign of directly influencing the priorities and principles informing decisions being made within the municipal chambers of towns and cities up and down the country; a campaign that would sow the seeds for a decade of growth in the status afforded to children's right to play by policymakers across the UK.

While the Charter was promoted and adopted as a whole, it was one of its principles in particular that was to have the greatest impact on emergent play policy. This was principle five: 'central and local government and voluntary organisations should think creatively and strategically about children and their play'. Having begun to win the argument in principle for greater recognition and better policy for play, the challenge now was to promote a feasible model for how to effectively plan for it: a model that could be adopted as government policy.

FOUR

'New opportunities'

Lottery funding and the beginnings of public play policy

When John Major made an election pledge (Conservative Party, 1992) to create a new National Lottery to raise money for good causes, he 'knew it was the only way we could fund a rebirth of cultural and sporting life in Britain' (Major, 1999). Children's culture is found in their play – indeed, it can be said that, in a sense, playing *is* children's culture (Fagen, 2005) – and so it is perhaps no surprise that this new way of raising public money was to have such a big role in the policy breakthroughs that were eventually to lead to a national play strategy.

Major was the Conservative Prime Minister with the unenviable task of succeeding Margaret Thatcher in 1990. Installed without a popular vote after an internal party coup against a national icon, and commonly caricatured as lacking the charisma and conviction that had been the hallmarks of his predecessor, Major was not expected to win the 1992 election against a resurgent Labour Party.

Under the leadership of the skilled and dynamic Welsh orator, Neil Kinnock, Labour had largely purged itself of the more radical elements of the party, such as the militant tendency (New Statesman, 2010), which had been blamed for keeping it from office during the 1980s. It was doing consistently well in opinion polls and was widely predicted to win (Crewe, 1993). However, after a campaign in which Major had cleverly played to the strengths of his everyman image – famously taking his arguments directly to the people by literally standing on a soapbox in town squares up and down the country – the Conservatives won a record fourth consecutive general election. That this time they did so not with the talismanic leader who had redefined her party and transformed the political and economic landscape of her country (even as she was dividing it) but with the diffident, somewhat nerdish Major, only underlined the extent to which the political centre of gravity had shifted to the right: a fact not lost on the pre-eminent young Labour modernisers, Tony Blair and Gordon Brown.

Like Thatcher, the perennial Conservative divisions would plague John Major over its relationship with the European Economic Community (EEC), as it was then. Along with a series of ministerial scandals that became known by the unwelcome collective noun 'government sleaze' and which hugely undermined his aims to refresh the party after the Thatcher years with his 'back to basics' policy relaunch, the party's infighting over Europe largely dominated his time in office (Bennett, 2012).

For many, including himself (Major, 1999), the National Lottery was John Major's greatest legacy. Established as he had promised by an Act of Parliament in 1993, this twice-weekly giant state raffle sees 28% of its ticket sales allocated via a number of different distributing bodies to a range of 'good causes'. From 1994 to 2007, this amounted to more than £15 billion of new funding for charities, sports, arts and heritage projects (Select Committee on Culture, Media and Sport, 2007). Major later described the impact of National Lottery funding as 'a revolution in leisure for a country that has always undervalued its free time' (Major, 1999). Our earlier discussions suggest that this is nowhere more true than in our attitude to children's play, and sure enough it was several years before Major's 'revolution' began to seriously benefit probably the most important leisure activity of them all.

With further irony, the lottery programme that would first demonstrate what dedicated play funding could do for children came from a development that John Major and his Conservative colleagues strongly opposed. The New Opportunities Fund (NOF), a lottery distributor launched by Culture Secretary Chris Smith in 1999 – two years after Tony Blair's landslide victory had ended 18 years of uninterrupted Tory rule and swept John Major from office – was created to enable lottery money to be directed specifically to initiatives in health, education or the environment. The controversy was that this appeared to break the 'additionality' rule: a key lottery principle (HM Government, 1992) that ensured its funds were not used for purposes that were the responsibility of government. However, while the Labour government was criticised – and not just by the opposition – for seeming to allow ministers to use lottery funding for their own pet projects, for the play movement it was less important who won this argument than that children's play provision should become one of them.

Ever since adventure playgrounds had begun to secure grants from their local councils and to apply for funding from charitable trusts, children's play providers had been required to explain themselves in terms of extraneous benefits in order to justify why they should receive money. From reducing young offending and increasing social cohesion to improving physical fitness and supporting out-of-school learning, depending on the funder, successful play projects were good at being all things to all people. The play movement would bite the outcomes bullet with the publication of Best Play (NPFA et al, 2000), but we needed funders to recognise that these outcomes were worth supporting. Mostly, we needed the simple result of more children playing more often to be considered a desirable outcome in its own right.

Around the same time that NOF was being created in 1999, CPC was awarded its government contract for national policy, research and information services. One consequence of this was that it became a body that agencies like NOF were expected to consult with. As such, at a CPC meeting in 2000 we were given a presentation by NOF officials who were keen to hear from us just exactly how it was that children's play provision could 'add value' to new programmes that they were developing. They knew of many play projects, they said, that had received funding from other lottery programmes. What were the important criteria of such projects that would lead to their optimum contribution to health, education and environmental outcomes? Seeing an opportunity, we tried to convey to our guests that good play provision can make a big contribution to the sorts of outcomes that they were seeking for children and therefore to the kind of programmes that they wanted to design, but that for optimum benefits they should really think about creating a distinct play programme that seeks only to support more children playing.

More often than not, when politicians or their officials are 'consulting', one knows by their response to contributions – sometimes just in their body language – that the exercise is little more than a token gesture; that decisions may not have been announced, but that they have effectively been taken. There is a suspicion that whatever they hear will be of no consequence. Other times, there is a clear sense that the exercise is real; that they genuinely want to receive more ideas and hear from different perspectives.

Against all our expectations, born of many years of being patronised or dismissed when advocating for serious public funding for play, the NOF officials at the Children's Play Council that day in 2000 seemed suddenly intensely interested. The discussion palpably changed gear. Far from going through the usual motions of presenting us with options that had in fact already been closed, they were engaged, probing the idea and its possibilities, asking real, intelligent questions and genuinely listening to our answers. It seemed like a penny had dropped – a large coin, from a great height – that had been waiting for its moment for a very long time. There was a buzz among the group and a keen sense that we should follow up this unexpected level of interest as quickly and helpfully as possible.

In the weeks after this meeting it became clear that our interpretation of the meeting was not an illusion. This new public funder, the lottery distributor most closely aligned with government policy, was evidently seriously interested in our suggestion that it create a national programme purely for children's play. More – and more detailed – consultations followed.

It is perhaps a common feature of successful policy advocacy that whoever makes the winning case may be quite likely to then be asked to help develop and implement it. Governments, it seems, adopt policy more than make it, and then need specialists to help them implement or deliver it. Be careful what you ask for. Thus it was that CPC – in partnership with the large national children's charity Barnardo's, a longstanding member of the council with the kind of capacity to deliver a nationwide programme – made the successful bid to become NOF's award partner for the £10.8 million Better Play programme (2001), England's first publicly funded national programme for children's play. Although a real milestone in the development of national play policy (especially in light of what was to follow), Better Play was, in fact, not a discrete funding programme in its own right but part of the £130 million Green Spaces and Sustainable Communities programme (Big Lottery Fund, 2008), enabling it to embrace as one its overall aims the challenge of 'creating and improving outdoor space for children's play', albeit on a somewhat modest scale. NOF's interest in a play programme was genuine enough, but the funder and its government masters evidently needed to explore the sector's potential before investing in a more substantial initiative.

A total of 225 different projects received funding over three different rounds from 2002-5. The initial broad aims of the programme, and the objectives that projects needed to meet, were:

- To produce opportunities for children to play safely within their neighbourhoods;
- To offer opportunities for community members to take part in providing good play opportunities for their children;
- To enhance the health and safety of children in disadvantaged neighbourhoods;
- To address the play needs of particularly disadvantaged groups within neighbourhoods;
- To support the development of local play policies and strategies.

After the first two rounds of funding, the delivery partners aged with the funder to dedicate the final round to promoting inclusive play provision based on the social model of disability, and allocating funds to projects – 94 in total – aiming for more disabled and non-disabled children to play together.

An important feature of the Better Play programme was that it adopted the playwork definition and also used the Best Play outcome objectives as a measure of the quality of the projects delivered. The programme also used a quality assurance system, Quality in Play (Conway and Farley, 2001) that placed these standards within a framework for self assessment and, potentially, external accreditation. These were the sort of things that Chris Smith (see page 65) had exhorted the sector to develop, and it was an indication that the government was keeping a close watch on how we responded to his challenge that he was happy to describe

Quality in Play, for example, as 'an important addition to the tools available to ensure good practice in this increasingly professional sector' (Smith, 2001)

In spite of certain shortfalls between the programme's aims and its evaluated outcomes (Youlden and Harrison, 2006), Better Play was widely perceived – including, crucially and very publicly, by the funder – to have 'delivered'. At a CPC event in 2005, NOF's Chief Executive Stephen Dunmore – now also head of the emerging Big Lottery Fund (see page 87) – called it 'an absolute triumph'. As it transpired, this resounding endorsement from the man in charge of the largest non-governmental funding body in history would prove to be immensely important for the next steps towards a national play policy.

Equally significant, though, was some of the work carried out under the smallest, fourth strand of the programme. Sowing the seeds for future policy work and providing some much-needed capacity for play advocates to take on the challenge of engaging local and regional policymakers, as well as the public sector professionals – whose cooperation would be necessary to seriously plan for play beyond the playground. This was the funding that NOF's Better Play programme made available for the development of play strategies, a concept whose time had come.

FIVE

'A vital and vibrant city'

How devolved government in London
set a benchmark for play policy

With a strong playwork tradition and more adventure playgrounds (Shier, 1984) and play associations than anywhere else in the country, it was perhaps no surprise that the big breakthrough for play policy in England occurred in London. However, there were political factors, unique to the capital, which were to have an equally significant bearing on events.

When New Labour won its landslide victory under Tony Blair in the general election of 1997, its policy on London contained something of a conundrum of realpolitik. Blair and his chancellor, Gordon Brown, had led an extensive modernising agenda with a more business-friendly political culture than previous Labour governments had a reputation for. For example, key Blairite, Peter Mandelson (cited in Wighton, 1998) declared the party to be 'intensely relaxed about people getting filthy rich, as long as they pay their taxes'. For the traditional party of the working class this was something of a departure and was to set Downing Street on a collision course with the heir apparent to the London throne.

In 1986, the Conservative government of Margaret Thatcher had abolished the Greater London Council (GLC), led by 'Red' Ken Livingstone, after which he became a champion of the left-wing of the Parliamentary Labour Party, standing against Tony Blair for the leadership after the sudden death of John Smith in 1994. Upon the party's 1997 victory it was no surprise, given his uncompromising stance on socialist principles, that Livingstone was passed over for ministerial duties. Just as he had been a *bête noire* for Prime Minister Margaret Thatcher – opposing everything she stood for from his alternative power base across the Thames – so he now became, this time from the backbenches, a thorn in the side of the Blair government; New Labour's *'Bête Rouge'* (Rawnsley, 2001). The conundrum for Blair was that Labour had opposed the abolition of the GLC and had an established policy to reinstate some form of devolved regional government for the capital: an authority that Ken Livingstone was widely regarded as the natural candidate to lead.

By 1999, Livingstone had become one of New Labour's most vocal internal critics and Blair was determined that he should not be Labour's official candidate. The Health Secretary, Frank Dobson, a long-serving London MP, was chosen instead, but Livingstone dramatically resigned from the party to stand as an independent candidate and won a resounding 57% of the vote. Dobson, who had been reluctant to stand in a contest, tainted by what many saw as a rigged Labour selection process, came a poor third after the Conservatives' Stephen Norris.

Ken Livingstone was to prove – certainly in his first term – a popular and highly influential Mayor of London (Butler, 2003) with innovative, largely successful policies on transport and planning in addition to his famed egalitarianism. His key role in the city's successful bid to host the 2012 Olympic Games, and the leadership he showed in the aftermath of the London terrorist bombings on 7 July 2005 – the day after the award of the Games (Livingstone, 2005) – even garnered him a kind of heroic national status. Long before those rollercoaster events, his reputation as an effective leader had been enhanced by his daring congestion charging policy for the city centre and his command of public transport. Far from his image as the dangerous champion of the 'loony left' painted by the right-wing tabloid press, Livingstone had got London moving again and played a key role in securing its reputation as one of the world's finest cities.

New Labour could no longer afford to cut off its political nose to spite its face and Livingstone was to rejoin the party in 2003. It was, however, during those early years as an independent Mayor with 'the largest and most direct mandate of any politician in British history' (Hosken, 2008) that, free of the need to toe a party line and with a brand new administration to run, he was both open to new ideas and most able to act on them.

Play advocates in London make a breakthrough

It was the Inner London Education Authority (ILEA) – responsible for youth provision and supporting children's play, as well as running schools in the inner London area – that had provided funding for the London Adventure Playground Association (LAPA). This was the independent charity, chaired in the 1960s by Lady Allen, that had done so much to strengthen the play movement in the city and to advance the good practice and professionalism of adventure playgrounds in particular (Raven, 1977). Although it retained some financial support from the voluntary sector funding body, London Borough Grants (LBG), with the loss of ILEA funding LAPA had been forced through the 1990s to pare back its direct support for adventure playgrounds and had begun to focus on policy and research. Crucially, it also broadened its geographical scope to become a national charity, changing its name to PLAYLINK. PLAYLINK produced some widely regarded publications, held national conferences and established an important role for itself within the national play movement. Its director Sandra Melville chaired the increasingly influential CPC and was a strong voice for playwork, adventure playgrounds and their often voluntary management structures on the Children's Play Policy Forum.[1]

In London, however, the adventure playgrounds and some of the borough-wide play associations that supported them locally were missing the presence of a specifically London-focused support body for the play sector. In 1995, some of them argued to PLAYLINK's main funder, LBG, that the play sector in the region still needed a strategic body: one that would focus uniquely on support and development for open access play provision and provide a collective voice for those campaigning for children's right to play in the capital. LBG responded by commissioning a review of the sector by the leisure management consultant, George Torkildsen. The Torkildsen report (1996) found that, while there were some boroughs providing a range

---

[1] This was a cross-sector group, supported by government funding and hosted by the Local Government Association (LGA), for leading play organisations to engage with government departments and agencies such as the Audit Commission.

of excellent play services and spaces, the majority were not. Local authority open access play provision, with no statutory basis (unlike youth services) even where it was relatively strong, was beginning to be squeezed out by the pressure on councils to increase support for registered childcare. There was also a trend away from local grant schemes towards contracted services, as the Thatcher government policy of introducing market mechanisms into public services found willing allies in those borough councils with Conservative majorities.

Across the London adventure playground network there was a big reliance on the voluntary sector: mainly small local management committees that struggled with the relatively more complex demands that came with increased regulation of the sector, under the 1989 Children Act. Until well into the 1990s, many adventure playgrounds operated with not even minimal administrative resources such as indoor office space, computers or dedicated finance staff. Within a growing contract culture that placed a heavy burden of monitoring and administration on them, this was a challenge that for many was unsustainable.

Torkildsen found that 'second-tier'[2] help for the front-line voluntary play sector was patchy. There were some good play associations – in boroughs like Islington and Hackney, which had a high concentration of adventure playgrounds – but these were few and far between. In general, the field lacked consistent infrastructure support and, since the demise of LAPA – or its transformation into PLAYLINK – many adventure playgrounds were left isolated and vulnerable. As well as the lack of regional infrastructure, Torkildsen also noted the dearth of a meaningful policy framework for play provision. His headline recommendation, as the play associations had hoped, was for the establishment of a new London-wide body to provide not only vital support and development capacity, but also a vehicle for the influencing and campaigning activity that would be needed to effect policy change.

In 1997, LBG responded to the Torkildsen Report by inviting a steering group of the city's play organisations – mainly play

---

[2] 'Second-tier' is the term, commonly used within the UK voluntary sector, to denote activities that are not directly for the target group, but to support those providing 'front-line' services to them.

associations from the boroughs, but also PLAYLINK and the London Voluntary Services Council (LVSC), which serviced the group – to develop plans for a new regional coordinating and support body for children's play, and to submit an application for a ringfenced grant. The embryonic London Play, as the new body would be called, was launched in Coram's Fields, central London, in the summer of 1997, before being awarded an LBG grant of £100,000 the following year. The capital's play movement once again had its own body, and a regional play policy was high on its agenda.

The advent (or return) of a regional government for London was one reason why the play movement in the capital had advocated so strongly for a new strategic vehicle. The London Play steering group knew that the policy context for open access provision was fraught with potential threats to the organic, grassroots movement that had seen adventure playgrounds proliferate in the 1960s and 1970s, and if not quite prosper under, then at least endure the Thatcher years.

As well as the challenge of the 'childcare revolution' (Smith and Baker, 2000), which was putting pressure on adventure playgrounds to change their ethos and offer registered places to fee-paying parents, the nascent charity knew that the wider barriers to London children's time and space to play were also growing. Ever increasing traffic, the density of inner city areas, poorly designed social housing, fear of crime and bullying and negative perceptions of children and young people in public space were just some of the factors conspiring to drive children from the streets that had been their traditional play domain for generations (Hood, 2001). London did not just need to protect and build more adventure playgrounds, it needed to address the problem of unaccompanied children disappearing from public space altogether. We knew that the challenge was to persuade the authorities to adopt long-term policies that would see London become a properly child-friendly city: 'a city where all children can play', as London Play aspired to in its mission statement.

With the award of a £350,000 lottery grant and some other fundraising successes, London Play grew quickly into the kind of organisation that could at least attempt to effectively highlight the changing play needs of London's children to policymakers. To exercise any real influence on the new Mayor, however, we knew we would need some allies; and during the first London Mayoral election campaign of 1999–2000, the Children's Rights Alliance for England (CRAE) was in the process of establishing a lottery-funded project in London that was to prove the perfect partner for our policy ambitions.

One of the several anomalies of British devolution was that Wales, Scotland and Northern Ireland each had their own statutory but independent Children's Rights Commissioners, while England's children were served in this capacity only by a government department. Believing that this had the effect of disadvantaging children in England relative to their peers in the other three nations, and acting as a brake on the whole children's rights agenda, CRAE aimed to make the case to the UK government for a rights commissioner for England's 11 million children. One of its tactics to this end was to establish a project in London that had the appearance of an official commissioner's office but was in fact a short-term project, funded by the National Lottery, with no official role but as free to campaign and lobby as any other charity. The ingeniously named Office of the Children's Rights Commissioner for London (OCRCL) was established in March 2000 with the purpose of demonstrating the value of such a role and its potential to influence government.

Children's rights, as such, were not a cause much embraced by mainstream British politicians in the 1990s – certainly not within the UK government. Eighteen years of Conservative rule had moved the political centre of gravity to the right, and although it was the Thatcher administration that ratified the UNCRC in 1989, the discourse about children was often less about their rights than about their perceived threat to law and order. Young people were becoming the subject of a moral panic as traditional values like discipline and deference were perceived to have been eroded by such phenomena as single parenthood, street culture and liberal approaches to education (Pilcher and Wagg, 1996). The popular, predominantly right-wing press was regularly filled with alarmist stories highlighting young people's delinquency, characterised by gangs of 'hoodies': the disparaging label now attached to teenagers, especially boys, after the ubiquitous hooded tops that they stereotypically wore (Marsh and Melville, 2006). In this narrative, children's rights were cast as part of the problem: a 'politically correct' indulgence that excused bad behaviour and was undermining the social order (Fortin, 2009).

Labour, in its 1997 victory, had staked a credible claim to the centre ground, including the assertion that it was the true party of law and order. Tony Blair (1993) had famously promised to be 'tough on crime, tough in the causes of crime' and this would include, especially, an uncompromising approach to the problem of 'feral youth' (Brown, 1998). His Home Secretary, Jack Straw, was to introduce legislation effectively criminalising young people's free association by making activities such as congregating in groups liable to new 'ASBOs': Anti Social Behaviour Orders[3] (Hughes, 2007), a term that became bound up with perceptions of disaffected young people and errant, out-of-control children, even though many of the most widespread incidences of anti-social behaviour – such as public drunkenness, football violence and rioting – were in fact mostly perpetrated by adults.

In the context of this popular demonisation of children and young people in public space – a phenomenon that would see high-frequency 'mosquito' buzzers, only audible to those under the age of 25, installed in shops and public places in order to drive them away (Squires, 2008) – even those vying for the centre ground of British politics were rarely to be heard speaking of children's rights without quickly qualifying the term. At an event in Parliament to launch CRAE's proposals for a Children's Commissioner for England, Cherie Blair, the Prime Minister's wife and human rights lawyer, said: "Whenever we talk about children's rights, it is important to consider their responsibilities too. There are no rights without responsibilities" (2003). This was a subject close to her husband's heart (Seldon, 2007) and a position enshrined by a Home Office (2003) White Paper on the matter that same year.

It was, therefore, a significant departure from the prevailing policy winds when Ken Livingstone published the London Strategy for Children and Young People (Mayor of London, 2004a), basing it squarely on the CRC. The importance of the rights-based approach

---

[3] ASBOs were quasi-judicial instruments – issued by local authorities, not the courts – for proscribing or constraining activities which, while not illegal, were nevertheless causing 'a nuisance' (Squires, 2008). Breaching an ASBO was illegal. Children could now be brought before the courts for simply congregating in groups or playing too loudly in the street if an ASBO had been issued to them to desist.

adopted by the London Mayor, especially for the prospects for play policy, cannot be overstated. The overarching national framework of universal outcomes for children – the Every Child Matters policy – would, initially, leave play out in the cold, (see Chapter Seven) in spite of children's own expressed wishes that it should be a top priority. However, the same year that Every Child Matters (ECM) would become law as the Children Act, 2004, the Mayor of London accepted that the case had been made for children's play as their human right; and that its provision was therefore a responsibility of government. Although evidence of how good play provision could help the realisation of better outcomes for children was part of the Mayor's (2005) guidance on planning for play to the London Boroughs, ensuring a strategic fit with the ECM framework, its defining aims and purpose, as well as its structure, were drawn directly from the CRC, thus affording children's play needs a much higher priority than was yet the case within UK government policy.

But there were two other, very different, factors that contributed to the play policy breakthrough in London. The first of these was to do with the extent – and the limits – of the powers that had been devolved to the Mayor. Although these were very considerable, including key areas like transport and police, as far as child policy was concerned there were considerable constraints on what the Greater London Authority (GLA) could actually do. Resisting calls for a return to the days of ILEA, the government had left schools under the control of the London boroughs, and with the wider domain of children's services now a subject of major reform (HM Treasury, 2003b) – not least to make them more integrated – it was not about to create a new regional tier of administration within a system that it already believed to be over complicated.

Thus, although the Mayor's children's strategy embraced the CRC in principle as a whole, it would need to focus on those children's rights most affected by government functions that fell within the new regional authority's remit. One of these was planning. The Mayor's overarching London Plan – the statutory spatial development strategy for the London region – was the key policy vehicle for the city, setting out 'a fully integrated economic, environmental, transport and social framework for the development of the capital' over 20 years. We knew that securing a policy for children's play within this vitally important, high-level strategy would enshrine the commitment within the overall vision for the city and open the door to further policy development. Here surely was a chance for Lady Allen's vision of a crosscutting, collaborative approach to the public realm, centred on liveable, playable spaces for children, to take root in a major administration. This was a real opportunity for children's play to be at the heart of the democratically mandated public vision for the capital city.

Before the first London Plan was adopted in 2004, there was an extensive consultation. This included the legal requirement for its 'examination in public', with calls for evidence at open hearings in City Hall, the Mayor and Assembly's base opposite the Tower of London on the South Bank of the Thames. Using a Better Play NOF grant (that we had argued at CPC should be available for just such a purpose), London Play engaged the planning specialists Arup to help submit a detailed case and give evidence to the hearings about the need to include a suitable policy for play within the London Plan.

The State of London's Children Report (SOLCR), an independent study of relevant research and data about the capital's children and young people, commissioned by the GLA (Hood, 2001), demonstrated how children and young people's independent access to the public realm has been increasingly restricted, principally on account of traffic and 'stranger danger'. It found that these restrictions had a stronger impact on London's children than those living elsewhere in England. The report also highlighted 'how the Article 31 rights of young Londoners have not been adequately met', with inequalities in access to play opportunities particularly affecting disabled children and those from minority communities.

The revised and updated SOLCR (Hood, 2004) was stronger still on the importance of play and the evidence of the pressures and barriers to London children's enjoyment of it. It said, 'opportunities for play are a critical and free resource for all young Londoners, but particularly for those on low incomes whose access to commercialised and costly play and recreation facilities may be limited [...] London's 10–14 year-olds were less likely than children in a town outside London, to be allowed to play in the street, ride a bike on the main road or walk alone to a friend's house.' The report warned that 'increasingly high land value sales have led, in London, to the sale of playing fields, playgrounds and open land

[...] often in inner London, where deprivation levels are higher, and where open spaces for children to play are already in short supply'. And it noted London Play's concerns that 'the government's recent policy emphasis [...] has meant that childcare, youth crime and child protection have dominated the policy agenda, with local authorities moving resources out of play provision and into services that meet centrally determined targets'.

Our policy case to the London Plan hearings was simply that, given this context and the Mayor's commitment to children's rights, an effective policy for children's play should be integral to the Plan's overarching aims 'to make London a better city for people to live in [...] to promote social inclusion [...] to improve its accessibility and to make it a more attractive, well-designed and green city'. Play provision itself, however, was not within the Mayor's powers. Like schools and other children's services, it was the responsibility of London's 33 local councils. The SOLCR, like the Torkildsen Report of 1996, had found that without any clear statutory basis or national policy framework, this provision and the funding allocated to it was highly variable. Although including play within the London Plan would send out a strong message, and the Mayor's planning powers would ensure that children's play was properly considered in major new developments, there would need to be other mechanisms to implement the policy at a local level.

The challenge of how to use the powers of a strategic regional authority like the London Mayor to develop a policy that would promote better play provision and more playable public space for children locally was resolved in the decision to issue two distinct guidance documents: one setting out the need and a recommended process for preparing local crosscutting play strategies; the other on the use of benchmark standards in the developments and provisions that would follow.

The London Plan (Mayor of London, 2004b) therefore included the following statement (Policy 3D.13):

> The Mayor will ensure that all children have safe access to good quality [...] play and informal recreation provision. Boroughs should produce strategies on

play [based on] audits of existing play and recreation provision.

This, quite possibly the first strategic play policy adopted by such a major authority anywhere in the world, was more succinctly captured in the summarised version of the Mayor's Strategy for Children and Young People (2004):

> The Mayor wants London to be a more child-friendly city [...] that respects the rights of children [...] making sure that public spaces [...] for children to play are not lost when places are being redeveloped, and that planners allow for these spaces when designing new developments.

To facilitate this new approach the Mayor commissioned London Play to produce his Guide to Preparing Play Strategies (2005). We then worked with the GLA, to transform Trafalgar Square into a giant playground for national Playday in August, where Livingstone used the occasion to reinforce his aims to create a child-friendly, playable capital city. "There should be high-quality provision for play in every neighbourhood," he said, "and this guide aims to provide a framework for developing local play opportunities within a regional context."

The Mayor had set out a bold vision, in which, contrary to the prevailing trends, children would not only have more and better play areas; they would also be better able to play in safer streets and routes to school and in public spaces designed with children in mind:

> Being able to have fun in public spaces and participate in cultural life is one of the hallmarks of a vital and vibrant city. Children need access to dedicated play space but also to child-friendly neighbourhood environments, green and open spaces. The play strategy should assess and analyse not just the quantity, quality and current usage of existing play spaces and facilities but the current accessibility of the public realm

against the needs and wishes of local children and young people. (Mayor of London, 2004a)

Along with the concurrent policy to offer all children and young people free public transport and therefore greater mobility, the Mayor was honouring their claim to a greater stake in the public realm of the city. It was a long-term vision to not simply improve play spaces, but to make other spaces playable too; to 'expand the areas of the public realm where all children and young people feel safe and welcomed' (Mayor of London, 2004a). Drawing on Jacobs (1961), this was the vision that Lady Allen (Hurtwood, 1968) had begun to paint decades earlier.

Like Lady Allen, however, we knew that for the vision to even begin to materialise would need a serious commitment from London's 33 local authorities – none of which owed any allegiance to the radical, independent Mayor of London. His statutory planning powers meant that they would have to give consideration to his guidance when making decisions on large-scale new developments, and that their Local Development Frameworks should now include references to local play strategies; but for these strategies to have any real impact, the London boroughs would need an incentive to increase their activity, their outputs and especially their spending on play. For the Mayor's vision to be adopted and manifested for London's communities, guidance alone would not be enough. The next steps towards an effective play policy, in London as much as the rest of the country, would need to include some dedicated new funding on a much larger scale than the £10 million Better Play Programme.

SIX

'Making the case'

The call for a national play strategy

By a coincidence of government restructuring, the department with responsibility for the National Lottery under the New Labour government of 1997 was also the one that had contracted CPC to deliver a small policy and research programme (HM Treasury, 2003). The Department for Culture, Media and Sport (DCMS) had inherited such responsibility for children's play as there was at that time within Whitehall from one of its predecessors, the Department for National Heritage.

There were two main problems with play policy residing at the DCMS. First, this placed it outside of the main locus for child policy – the Department for Education and Employment – which, especially under New labour, was to very explicitly broaden its reach and ambition to drive up improvements in every area of children's lives touched by public services or the public realm (HM Treasury, 2003). Second, it simply did not have the budget to promise any substantial changes to an area of public life as universal as children's play. It was an 'arm's length' funder of the arts and sport, and also managed the government's relationship with the BBC.

Nevertheless, the DCMS is where play policy resided. Fortunately, the department also had two saving graces as far as the play movement was concerned. The first of these was that the lottery distributors were accountable to it, and to some degree took their policy direction from it – especially in the case of NOF (see Chapter Four). The second was Culture Secretary, Chris Smith.

A couple of years before the CPC meeting with NOF, in October 1998, the Secretary of State was invited to speak at London Play's first annual meeting. As an Islington MP renowned for his support of local action, the minister was a long-term friend of the Islington Play Association and the 12 adventure playgrounds in the Borough. He accepted our invitation and the event was a huge success, sending out a message that the 'new kid on the block' in London meant business (and so impressing our funding officer from London Boroughs Grants that he immediately took us off the 'high-risk' category!).

More important than the kudos for London Play, however, was the substance and tone of Smith's speech. Clearly well-informed and empathetic with the play movement from his long association with IPA, he delivered an address that was not only knowledgeable and sensitive to our issues, but also challenging and promising in equal measure. Recognising the vital significance of play in children's lives here and now as well as its value to their health and development, the Culture Secretary said: 'I cannot think of anything else that offers so much to children [...] play is not only important to [their] quality of life [...] it is of great importance for our country's future, to the creative industries and for the economy'. He said that the play sector had an important role, which, as Secretary of State, he wanted to support. First though, he wanted to give us three challenges: 'develop and adopt agreed outcomes for good play provision; create a recognised training and qualifications framework; and speak with one voice. Do this and I will be listening'.

Over the two year period after Chris Smith's challenges in 1999, a momentum built for the sort of policy changes that had hitherto seemed out of reach. The movement itself had grown the kind of infrastructure and representational bodies that saw it increasingly referred to as a 'sector'. This was a mixed blessing but it entailed a maturity of sorts. The sector would struggle for years to reach a settled consensus on what the implied 'professionalisation' of playwork should involve (and arguably never has), but the incentive to respond to the government was great and led to a number of collaborative reports and statements about what we did broadly agree upon.

Over this period of codification, documents such as a Playwork Code of Conduct and a statement of the Assumptions and Values of Playwork paved the way for the emergence of the recognised National Occupational Standards (Skillsactive, 2010), seen by some as an essential part of the formalisation that would lead to better recognition of playwork and increased demand and resources for playwork services. There were others who felt that the rapidly accelerating 'professionalistion' of what had been an organic, intuitive way of working with children was leading to its institutionalisation within the pervading instrumental paradigm.

A key document in the sector's attempt to manage this tension was our collective response to Smith's call for an agreed set of intended outcomes for playwork services: 'Best Play: what play provision should do for children' (NPFA et al, 2000). Produced in a show of unity by a partnership between the NPFA, PLAYLINK and CPC, Best Play was explicitly framed as 'a response to the direct challenge issued by Chris Smith, for the field to work together to develop a statement of the benefits which are derived from play and play provision'.

The quid pro quo, calling on the government to deliver its side of the bargain, was to claim 'the publication shows that a body of knowledge has accumulated which allows the fundamental need for children's play to be asserted, bringing with it a commitment to the view that there should be public provision of high quality environments suitable for play' (NPFA et al, 2000). The responsibility for making such a commitment was placed squarely within the prevailing policy context of the National Childcare Strategy and was, in effect, a direct challenge to this rapidly growing area of state – or state-subsidised – out-of-school provision to be something that met the needs of children themselves as much as parents and employers.

Best Play did not have quite the influence on the 'childcare revolution' that some of us aspired to – the play movement's voice was small within a burgeoning industry that was being subsidised by the taxpayer not, for all the rhetoric, to improve the quality of children's lives so much as to allow their parents to go to work (Wilkinson, 1999) – but it was a vital document nonetheless. Tackling head-on the perennial conundrum of how to define the aims, objectives and outcomes of play provision without subverting the case for children's right to play for its own sake, the document adopted a definition of play that held the duality of 'freely chosen, personally directed, intrinsically motivated behaviour' through which 'children learn and develop as individuals, and as members of the community' as interdependent rather than conflicting facets. It also set out some of the evidence of the consequences for children of play deprivation, including their 'lower levels of physical activity, poorer ability to deal with stressful or traumatic situations [...] [and] poorer social skills'.

The key to children accruing benefits from play provision, as set out by Best Play, was that first and foremost they should be supported and enabled to 'extend the choice and control that [they] have over their play, the freedom they enjoy and the satisfaction they gain from it'. Supplementary to the primary principles of self-determination and enjoyment were three other 'immediate' objectives, namely that 'the provision: recognises the child's need to test boundaries and responds positively to that need; manages the balance between the need to offer risk and the need to keep children safe from harm; and maximises the range of play opportunities'. By regularly delivering these first four objectives, Best Play asserted that there was good evidence that, over time, provision could be expected to 'foster' some longer-term outcomes for children (objectives 5–7 in the list below). Along with offering 'opportunities for social interaction', these were 'independence and self esteem; respect for others; well being, healthy growth and development; and knowledge and understanding, creativity and [the] capacity to learn'.

Best Play squared the circle of defining outcomes for the staffed play sector in a way that did not feel like a compromise on its most essential principles. It made clear the distinction between play, which has no direct outcome, and play provision, whose primary outcome is children playing. Other benefits, it asserted, are 'fostered' (not guaranteed) only as a concomitant consequence of fulfilling this core purpose. This was a fundamental statement of intent. Within an arena dedicated to marshalling huge public resources to teaching, shaping and moulding children to be better equipped to join the adult world, while simultaneously corralling and protecting them from it, Best Play brought children's own agency – their deep need for a domain where they could exercise their own choices and make their immediate lives as children the priority – to the centre of the stage. It made an assertive and persuasive 'case for public investment in play' (NPFA et al, 2001).

There were protracted, not to say heated debates – and at least one substantial late redrafting of the manuscript – prior to arriving at a finished text for Best Play that the sector could rally around. But now we had a document that would enable government – and other potential funders – to see how it could contribute to their wider agenda for children. The suggested indicators for monitoring the seven objectives needed more work, but the sector had achieved what many had not thought possible: an agreed national framework, recognised by the government, for defining and evaluating the outcomes of our work.

Best Play Outcome Objectives

1. The provision extends the choice and control that children have over their play, the freedom they enjoy and the satisfaction they gain from it.
2. The provision recognises the child's need to test boundaries and responds positively to that need.
3. The provision manages the balance between the need to offer risk and the need to keep children safe from harm.
4. The provision maximises the range of play opportunities.
5. The provision fosters independence and self-esteem.
6. The provision fosters children's respect for others and offers opportunities for social interaction.
7. The provision fosters the child's well-being, healthy growth and development, knowledge and understanding, creativity and capacity to learn. (NPFA et al, 2000)

The argument for a national play strategy

After the London Play event, Chris Smith candidly let it be known that he wanted to consider potential alternatives to NPFA as the Government's voluntary sector partner for play policy. Of all the other organisations in the field, the CPC approach of roundtable membership discussions, forming policy positions and informing its plans, seemed to offer the best opportunity for the sector to be seen to be responding to his challenge that we should work together. It also, by that time, had a credible record within government for its leading work in the Department of Transport's Home Zones policy, aiming to model some of Britain's most spatially deprived residential areas on the Dutch *woonerf*, using 'shared space' street designs that gave right of way to pedestrians – including playing children – rather than vehicles.

London Play was in the majority of CPC members who argued that a national body comprising an active membership of other play organisations was exactly what the Secretary of State had called for, but that it could only be as strong as the capacity that it had to act, and as influential on policy development as its links into government made possible. The council agreed that our alliance would be little more than a talking shop unless our collective voice had the means to engage more with government.

CPC accepted the subsequent invitation to tender for the government contract, but before doing so, an important session of the council determined that our bid should have a new element. The NPFA role had been largely about collating and disseminating information; a conduit for cascading policy and practice news through the sector. Our aim was to change policy and improve practice and to build an evidence base of the state of play opportunities in the country that would highlight the need for government action. So it was that the Children's Play Council was awarded a government contract in 2000 that included a specific policy and research element. To their great credit, the NPFA remained a valued member, enabling us to genuinely represent the consensus view. Chris Smith had his united voice for the sector, although it is not entirely clear that he was ready for what we were to tell him.

CPC's *Making the case for play* (Cole-Hamilton and Gill, 2002) was one of the most important documents published in the long campaign for a proper UK government response to children's right to play. Confirming the fears identified in London by Torkildsen (1996) and the subsequent *State of London's children* report (Hood, 2001), the research found that there were many restrictions to children's play opportunities, including parental anxiety, poor maintenance and an often inadequate number of play spaces. In some areas, fee-charging childcare had replaced previously open access play provision, thereby excluding poorer children. The research also found that risk aversion was rife, with excessive health and safety concerns leading to unnecessary curtailment of adventurous play.

Most significantly, as far as calling for national action was concerned, the CPC research highlighted the wide disparity of opportunity experienced by children in different locations. While the factors creating barriers to children playing outside were common across the country – with some variations between rural, urban and suburban neighbourhoods – the responses of different local areas varied greatly. Fewer than 40% of local authorities had any kind of written play policy or service plan, let alone an area-wide or crosscutting strategy. In general the funding for play provision was poor, with 'little coordination or planning' and a disproportionate expenditure of capital investment on 'short-term pilot or start-up projects with little thought being given to long-term sustainability'.

CPC estimated that the average spend by local authorities on children's play provision was less than 7p per child per week, but with very great disparities in this per capita expenditure between different areas. The report found many authorities spending as little as a tenth on play provision compared to those spending the most. Unsurprisingly, there were also wide variances in the quality of provision and workforce development, with the research finding only one in three staffed play services having quality assurance, and no consistency in the training and qualifications for staff. 'A Postcode Lottery for Play' was the headline of CPC's press release to launch the document, and the solution to some of us seemed clear: that, with such a disparate picture, and generally low level of investment in provision, there needed to be a national play strategy.

With the benefit of hindsight, there is an argument that CPC could have argued for legislation in 2002. Other than as part of the extra-curricular responsibilities identified under the Education Act (1996), there was no statutory duty for local authorities to provide for children's play according to locally determined priorities. Our report showed that this approach was failing many children, who cannot vote, lobby or advocate for change. Why not, then, ask for a change in the law so that it was no longer discretionary for councils to provide play spaces and play services for their children?

There were some who argued for this, but they were not in the majority. The main reason against making play provision a statutory duty was that it was a crosscutting issue, needing the collaborative cooperation of many different departments and functions. The Charter for Children's Play had made clear that we considered children's right to play to be germane to all areas of their lives, needing a response from all parts of the public realm. Housing, streets, traffic and police, as well as parks and open spaces, schools and childcare – and of course dedicated play space, staffed and unstaffed – each had a role in children having time, space and opportunity to play, or not. The feeling was that it would be difficult to define these various responsibilities in law. Capturing the mosaic of different responsibilities across any given area within one piece of legislation seemed impossible. Attempting it, we felt, ran the risk of Parliament adopting too narrow a vision, enabling local authorities to meet a prescription for a limited type of service while reneging on their wider responsibilities.

Rather than, as we concluded, the blunt instrument of legislation, *Making the Case for Play* set out the rationale for a multifaceted, multi-tiered national framework to drive local action on play. The report's key proposal was that 'Government departments should work with the play sector to develop a National Strategy for Play – along the lines of the National Childcare Strategy – which identifies targets for local play provision based on an assessment of the needs and wishes of children and their communities'. While a national government strategy may have been the now clearly defined policy goal of the play movement – seen as the best way to remove the 'postcode lottery' of where and to what extent children enjoyed their right to play – it would again be the National Lottery itself that provided the injection of funds necessary to take the next major steps in the development of play policy in England.

SEVEN

'Things to do, places to go?'

How play was overlooked by children's services reform

Margaret Thatcher's Conservative administration of the 1980s, which had seen mass unemployment result from the restructuring of Britain's industrial economy, refused to concede that poverty existed in Britain. But while there was no official recognition and therefore no accepted definition of it during those years, academic research (Piachaud and Sutherland, 2001) showed that, by the most widely recognised measure (living below half of the mean level of income after housing costs), 'over the course of Conservative governments from 1979 to 1997 the number of children in poverty tripled' to 4.5 million: one in three of the child population. With the advent of the New Labour government of 1997, poverty – and child poverty in particular – became a major policy theme and, in March 1999, Prime Minister Tony Blair announced that 'our historic aim [is] to be the first generation to end child poverty [...] It is a 20 year mission' (White, 1999).

As we have seen, before the election that brought him to power, Blair had identified 'education, education, education' (Adonis, 2012) as his 'three' top priorities. However, while raising academic attainment may have been the Prime Minister's most favoured means for achieving his hugely ambitious goal on child poverty, there was a strong push from his influential Chancellor, Gordon Brown, to look at other causes of poverty and what else the government could do to alleviate them. The Chancellor was particularly interested in how economic inequality led to social exclusion, and what could be done for children who were at risk from it. His big initiative on this front was the Children's Fund, a national programme of investment in preventative, or 'upstream', projects and services 'over and above those provided through mainstream statutory funding' (Edwards et al, 2006). The initiative aimed to 'provide support for young people and their families before they reach crisis, while reducing the future probability of poor outcomes, and maximising life chances'. It was funded directly by the Treasury via an innovative cross-departmental Children and Young People's Unit (CYPU) to the projected tune of £780 million from 2001–8.

The Children's Fund redefined 'children in need' to include those 'at risk of social exclusion' and was specifically designed to 'engage and support voluntary and community organisations in playing an active part [in working] together to help children overcome poverty and disadvantage' (CYPU, cited in Morris et al, 2009). Children's Fund partnerships, independent of their local authorities, were tasked with developing plans for 'effective collaborative working to address the needs of children and young people, linked to education, health, antisocial behaviour, user involvement and capacity building'.

From the play movement's perspective, these high-level aims appeared to offer little opportunity. There was no mention of the vital role of play in building children's resilience, or of play services in providing space where children could thrive within otherwise deprived communities. At the Children's Fund launch in Whitehall in 2000, however, the two projects showcased to exemplify the kind of work it was aiming to support made us think again.

The first was Kids Company. This was a unique charity running a centre for children and young people in the deprived inner city suburb of Peckham in south London. Notwithstanding the problems that it would run into much later, causing its closure in 2015, Kids Company at that time had a reputation for engaging and working with children who were otherwise classed as 'hard to reach': excluded from school, in trouble with the police, 'looked after' by local authorities or living on the streets. The charity's charismatic founder and Chief Executive, Camilla Batmanjelidh, told the audience how these children were not hard to reach at all but all too commonly present: in the courts, hospitals, police cells and young offenders institutions of the capital. It was the services that were supposed to help them that were hard to reach, she said. Impersonal, bureaucratic institutions, case conferences and referral meetings were anathema to a troubled and vulnerable young person. The 'homes' in which they were 'looked after' were often as threatening to them as the abusive or neglectful family backgrounds from which they needed refuge. Kids Company worked, she claimed, because children were not referred to it; they found their own way there. This meant the place had to be recognisably part of young people's own culture: somewhere that attracted them. And so she had employed the most identifiable role models for street-smart young people in Peckham: the DJs and MCs from the local music clubs and sound systems, training them in person-centred counselling skills so as to create a community of young people and their mentors that was both cool and safe (in all senses of the word).

The second project presented to the assembled (and, by now, highly attentive) gathering of children's professionals at the Children's Fund launch was an adventure playground, the Venture (discussed in Chapter Two), which had evidently attracted the attention of policymakers because of its success at attracting not only children but also their families, who had come to rely on it as a hub of support in an area of high deprivation. Memorably, a teenage girl spoke movingly about how she had started going to the Venture even before starting school, and how it had become 'like a family' to her when things at home had become difficult and her parents had separated.

These two projects were very different, but had some strikingly similar themes. Playwork is not therapy, but a child-centred approach, reflective practice, and the principles of acceptance and empowerment are as important to good playwork as they are to counselling. An adventure playground like the Venture, far from being merely a maze of homemade structures for different kinds of locomotor play, was as much a community as the Kids Company centre in Peckham. Furthermore, a key to the success of each project was that they were 'open access': children were not referred by professionals but simply showed up looking for something, and so the projects had to embody children's own culture or they would vote with their feet. For this to happen, the staff in each place were trained to respond, not to direct; to enable, not to lead; and to always honour and respect the children and young people to whom they were in service. The key to these projects, from the perspective of a major government policy initiative to tackle social exclusion, was that they were each able to receive and engage children – and, in the Venture's case, often their families too – for whom other services did not work. The culture of acceptance – of boundaries negotiated, not imposed; of mutual respect, not authoritative rules; staffed by loving, responsible adults – was one that could be seen to provide children with that most vital element in their lives: a place of safety.

Until the Venture was put in the government's spotlight in this way, conceiving of play projects as 'interventions' for children in need or at risk had been problematic (and not everyone was happy about it now). Open access play provision is, by definition, universal: anyone within the appropriate age range can attend, whether 'in need' or not. But here was the Children's Fund, recognising the value of projects situated in areas of high deprivation with open door policies so that children could access them by their own initiative, and highlighting adventure playgrounds as an example. That the government had included an adventure playground as an exemplar of the work that it wanted to promote as part a flagship initiative was a tonic for a play sector otherwise feeling under siege from the pervasive influence of the National Childcare Strategy. Our newfound optimism would prove to be well founded, as play projects became important providers for many of the local Children's Fund Partnerships that followed. The national evaluation of the Children's Fund by Birmingham University (Edwards et al, 2006)found that as well as 'services [being] orientated around explicit communities of interest', they were also designed 'around key themes', and that play was typically one of these.

The role of play in building children's resilience and adaptability had long been recognised by paediatricians and psychologists, and is of course a tenet of play therapy, but this was possibly the first time it had been identified by an authoritative study of the impact of universal services for children at risk. Some play theorists and practitioners had identified that play deprivation was a serious issue (NPFA et al, 2000) giving rise to long-term problems for children who had to endure it. Now, a national evaluation of a major government programme, if not exactly stressing the point in the way that play campaigners might, was at least recognising play provision as having a valid and useful role in the range of 'protective factors [...] that reduce the child or young person's vulnerability to risk' (Edwards et al, 2006). As well as the direct benefits of free play for children needing opportunities to build their confidence and self-esteem, the Children's Fund evaluation also recognised the value of open access play projects in signposting children to other services. It highlighted, as an example, the work of one 'play centre in developing a playwork ethos of universal access within which there was attention to individual needs that may require specific interventions' (Edwards et al, 2006).

By the start of New Labour's second term in office (2001–5), it had become clear to the leadership that its ambitions to end child poverty and social exclusion could not be tackled by a one-off initiative, but needed comprehensive reform. In 2001, the government launched a major consultation to begin work on a 'radical [...] overarching strategy covering all services for children and young people' (CYPU, 2001). With playwork services featuring so unexpectedly prominently in the Children's Fund, play advocates were hopeful that the government's broader policy aims for children would now also present opportunities for play provision to secure better recognition and more opportunities to secure public funding. There were, initially, grounds for at least cautious optimism. The consultation document for the new approach (CYPU, 2001) set out ten unarguable principles; proposing, for example, that all children and young people's services should be 'centred on the needs of the young person [...] of high quality [and] [...] coherent in design and delivery'. There were further 'core principles for children and young people's participation in Government [...] to improve the extent to which children and young people impact on Government policy and services'.

The biggest innovation, however, was the government's intention 'to place a new emphasis on real life outcomes in children and young people's lives'. The proposal was for 'services to be designed and judged according to their ability to improve [...] lives' as demonstrated by 'meaningful well-being indicators'. These 'tangible improvements' were to be assessed within an outcomes framework 'reflecting the Government's aspirations for all children and young people [...] and encompassing all the key aspects of their lives'. The framework provisionally defined these outcomes within six areas:

1. Health and well-being
2. Achievement and enjoyment
3. Participation and citizenship
4. Protection
5. Responsibility
6. Inclusion.

Although none of these proposed outcomes included a direct reference to play, it was otherwise moderately well featured within the framework. Under *health and well-being*, for example, part of the government's aspiration for children and young people was that 'they should have the resilience, capacity and emotional well-being that allows them to play, learn, relate to other people, and resolve problems in life'. Under *achievement and enjoyment*, the aspiration was that 'children and young people should have the opportunity to fulfil their personal goals and ambitions [...] to achieve success in their academic, social and cultural development [...] and have the means to engage in constructive play and leisure pursuits for their own sake'. Some of us who had attended government workshops to assist in the drafting of the strategy grimaced a little when we read this last piece. The officials had clearly taken on board our exhortations that children had a right to play for its own sake, but had failed to understand how the term 'constructive play and leisure pursuits' somewhat failed to capture what we meant.

With participation and empowerment being such key themes of the proposed strategy, the Department for Education and Skills was duty bound by its own principles to consult on it as fully as possible with children themselves; of the 25 events held between December 2001 and March 2002, 12 of them were 'specially designed for children and young people to participate in' (CYPU, 2001). There was also a child-friendly version of the consultation document, with its own question and response forms. Curiously, rather than the six categories proposed in the draft strategy, children and young people were probed for their response to a different list. They were asked a range of questions about *seven* areas of their lives, including, specifically, which of these areas was most important (McAuley, 2010). These were:

1. Health
2. Leisure
3. Achievement
4. Crime
5. Environment
6. Families
7. Communities.

The results made interesting reading. By large majorities, children ranked leisure and their families as the top priorities. Under the leisure section of the survey, primary school children wanted 'more activities' and 'more parks' the most; secondary school children asked for 'more places to go'. Overall, 81% of children said they needed more play and recreational facilities. In contrast, when asked specifically how important 'better education' was to them, both groups ranked it as only their fifth most important priority. Far from 'education, education, education', when asked what most mattered to them, children were saying 'play, play, play'.

How the government responded to the results of the consultation on its proposed Children and Young People's strategy was to be influenced most not by the nonconformist preferences of the children who had participated in its roadshow, or indeed by any of the many hundreds of written responses it received from practitioners, academics and agencies from across the children's sector, but by a single tragic event: the 'slow, lonely death' of a terribly abused nine-year-old girl called Victoria Climbié (Laming, 2003).

The case of Victoria Climbié shocked the nation, not only because of the unspeakably cruel and degrading punishment of a sweet, vivacious child, but also because the services designed to protect children like her had evidently failed. Lord Laming's inquiry into these failings took almost two years to complete, with the Health Secretary and the Home Secretary jointly presenting their final report to Parliament in February 2003. The conclusions were a damning indictment of the local child protection agencies, detailing 'no fewer than 12 key occasions when [...] either police, health or social services had the opportunity to successfully intervene'. Lord Laming described their 'sloppy and unprofessional performance' as 'a gross failure of the system', the result of a 'widespread organisational malaise', which 'must change' (Laming, 2003).

The Laming Report contained 108 recommendations, including the principle that all services working with children and young people should be integrated within a common frame of reference and share information about vulnerable children. This should be managed within a common vision and a joint plan for children's services, coordinated at a senior level within local authorities.

Together with the concept of universal outcomes, this grand plan for a more integrated children's workforce offering a 'joined up' approach under an overall Directorate of Children's Services that would include health, education and social care was to become the long-term strategy and overarching policy for children and young people that became known as Every Child Matters (ECM). Published first as a Green Paper[1] in 2003, ECM was as much the government's response to the Laming Report as the result of its wider deliberations and consultations on a long-term strategy for children and young people. Although the outcomes framework was still the overarching theme, it was the reform of statutory services to create the cohesive, integrated network of professionals ready to respond to children at risk that was now at the heart of the reforms.

Another change from the original proposals was that the Green Paper did not set out the six outcomes of its original consultation – or indeed the seven areas that children had been asked to prioritise. As everyone who worked in any capacity for children in England during the New Labour years knows, Every Child Matters identified five universal outcomes for children:

1. Being healthy
2. Staying safe
3. Enjoying and achieving
4. Making a positive contribution
5. Achieving economic wellbeing.

---

[1] A Green Paper in UK policy terms is a consultation document, setting out proposals and seeking responses to them, rather than a final plan.

The preferences of children themselves for more and better opportunities for play and recreation – and a greater freedom to enjoy their own social and cultural lives – so clearly expressed in their responses to the government's own consultation with them were covered in barely a paragraph of the Green Paper, which acknowledged that children and young people wanted more 'things to do and places to go' (HM Treasury, 2003). The document neglected to say how this was to be achieved, or what role the government would play in achieving it. In fact, the policy had so little to say about play and recreation that for months and even years after ECM was published, ministers and officials could be heard talking about the third outcome not as 'enjoying and achieving', but 'enjoying achieving'.

A closer reading of the document and its supplements confirms that 'enjoying' was intended to refer not only to school, but also to children's play and recreational lives too. Nevertheless, an insight into the dominant strain of government thinking was perhaps better conveyed by Children's Minister Margaret Hodge, who, when challenged about the lowly position of play under the 'enjoy and achieve' part of the framework, told an NCB conference soon after the policy's launch: 'I think children do enjoy school and, anyway, we do not think that for them there is any real difference between play and learning.' The ECM outcomes were habitually presented as those that 'mattered most' to children and they were soon accepted as a given part of the child policy landscape. Although the play element in the policy was widely misinterpreted and underdeveloped, the challenge for CPC and other play advocates was how to engage with policymakers in a way that could turn this around.

At this stage, CPC's capacity for campaigns, communications and policy work was limited. As a small membership body with an even smaller central hub, even with NCB''s support we knew that if we were to strengthen the calls for a national play policy we would need to grow significantly. In the meantime we agreed to use allies to amplify the play message, which included an approach to the newly renamed 4Children (formerly KCN: Kids Clubs' Network), an organisation that seemed to be growing in capacity and influence each year as the National Childcare Strategy gathered pace.

4Children's Chief Executive, Anne Longfield, had historical links with CPC, being instrumental in the council coming together and receiving its first government contract (she had been the embryonic body's treasurer during its formative years). More importantly, 4Children was very well connected with the government and had a large network of out-of-school providers: two benefits that we needed to take advantage of. Working with 4Children was a controversial tactic; CPC members were not easily convinced that we should. This was partly because of 4Children's links with the food giant Nestlé, a company boycotted by many in the children's sector over its marketing of baby milk formula in the developing world; and partly because of their predominant role as the government's main partner for the childcare strategy, which many play practitioners believed was promoting a form of provision not in children's interests. Nevertheless, 4Children, with its growing network of after-school clubs and its leading role in one of the Labour government's flagship policies, was an organisation that we knew could help us to reach a wider audience and increase our influence.

So it was that, in June 2005, CPC and 4Children jointly staged what was probably the largest national play conference yet held in the UK. With 4Children's influence, the event was able to secure the new Children's Minister, Beverley Hughes, as the keynote speaker: a real opportunity to raise the profile of play as a policy issue and put pressure on the government to look again at Every Child Matters. What we had not had anticipated was that Helen Goodman, the Chief Executive of the National Association of Toy and Leisure Libraries, who was CPC's new chair, would by then have already resigned the position, having been elected to Parliament for the Labour Party at the general election just a few weeks earlier. Thus the conference was addressed not just by a key new minister, but also our newest and closest political ally.

The 'Playing Together' conference was a big success, with news of the emerging Lottery programme and one of Beverley Hughes's first speeches as Minister for Children ensuring a big attendance. The Minister pledged to ensure that children's play remained 'prominent' in the government's thinking and assured us that she would 'build it into the wider policy agenda' (Hughes, 2005). Nevertheless, some of us were not wholly convinced. While her engagement with the field was welcome, her description of play 'as a vehicle for learning and development and a route to better outcomes' confirmed how far we still had to go to persuade the government that it was an area in need of its own policy, with its own rationale.

Nevertheless, it was now clear that children's play was now on the radar of the New Labour policy machine. Although not formally announced until 5 April 2005, exactly a month before it was held, the general election that the government hoped would see it returned for an historic third term of office had been expected for several months. Although the unprecedented flurry of Whitehall activity around the subject of children's play before and after the publication of Dobson's report had led to the government actually distancing itself from what would now be a decision of the Big Lottery Fund, the spin-doctors in Downing Street were nevertheless keen to invest whatever political capital could be made from the issue into Labour's campaign for reelection.

CPC's leading role in the review, and our ongoing discussions with BIG about a new programme, meant that we were no longer banging on a closed door as far as engagement with government policy was concerned. This unaccustomed 'insider' status was brought home to me when NCB, already very well connected with the New Labour government,[2] invited us to submit some proposals to the team drafting the party's election manifesto. Naturally, we suggested a promise to deliver on our by now longstanding call for a national play strategy, and were subsequently disappointed when the document seemed to promise nothing more than had already been agreed: 'Together with £155 million from the Big Lottery Fund, the Government will ensure that children who have had little access to play facilities and those with a disability have much better access to safe, modern playgrounds' (Labour Party, 2005). Nevertheless, this was the first time that children's play had been specifically included in an election manifesto of one of the main political parties. That it was the incumbent party meant that Downing Street now had play on its agenda.

---

[2]   NCB's Chief Executive, Paul (later Sir Paul) Ennals, was the son of former Labour Social Services Secretary, David Ennals, and a family friend of several ministers in the Blair administration, with whom NCB held a major strategic contract.

EIGHT

'Getting serious'

The national play review

Chris Smith may or may not have expected the sector that he had cajoled into speaking with one voice to be quite so demanding with it. A crosscutting national government play strategy, the main recommendation of CPC's *Making the case for play* (Cole-Hamilton and Gill, 2002), was certainly not on the reform agenda of the Department for Education and Skills (DfES), and Smith's own Culture Department (DCMS) was hardly concerned with children at all.

In the event, it was no longer his problem. By the time the CPC report was published, Smith had left the government, reshuffled out of office by a victorious Tony Blair immediately following the 2001 general election. But whatever the (soon to be ex-) Secretary of State may have imagined landing on his desk in the way of policy asks from the play movement, he proved uncommonly true to his word.

Smith had in various ways commended CPC, and the sector in general, for our robust response to his challenges. As though anticipating his imminent departure from the government and wanting to leave us something substantial to work with, completely out of the blue, on the very eve of the general election of June 2001, he issued a Labour Party news release pledging a further £200 million from the New Opportunities Fund (NOF) for children's play. The promised land of serious national investment for play seemed suddenly within reach.

Chris Smith's departing gift to the nation's children went unnoticed and unreported in a mainstream media understandably more interested in the wider implications of a second landslide election for Tony Blair and New Labour. More worryingly, no one at the DCMS, let alone NOF, appeared to have any knowledge of the pledge either. On hearing about the departure of our champion from the cabinet, anxious that the promise of funding (which only existed, as far as we were aware, in the form of a faxed Labour Party press release) would be deniable –by NOF, the government or both – and also wanting to publicly record our gratitude to the outgoing Secretary of State, we hastily penned a letter to *The Guardian* (Voce, 2001) warmly welcoming 'a legacy to the second-term government that New Labour can be proud of'. Meanwhile, we had no option but to wait patiently for a sign that the cabinet changes were not going to immediately nullify this sudden and unexpected breakthrough.

Chris Smith's successor as Culture Secretary was the MP for Dulwich, Tessa Jowell, a committed Blairite who had been a junior minister at the Department for Education and Employment. With no previous links to the play sector, and inheriting a portfolio bulging with issues about the government's policy direction over some of the nation's greatest obsessions (television, sport and gambling) (Brown, 2001), it would be many months before she would turn to the less pressing question, as it must have seemed at the time, of how the government should respond to children's growing need for somewhere to play. When Tessa Jowell eventually responded to CPC's persistent enquiries about how the government would take forward the agenda set out in *Making the case for play* and, more immediately, deliver on her predecessor's promise of a lottery programme for play, there was unintended irony in her chosen response. As related in Chapter Four, Ken Livingstone's incumbency as the first Mayor of London had brought an unprecedented policy focus to the question of children's play and it was to his beaten rival for the job, the former Labour Health Secretary, Frank Dobson MP, that the Secretary of State now turned.

Before entering Parliament in 1979, Dobson had been a leader of Camden Council, one of the inner London boroughs with a strong tradition in staffed play provision, and he was the long-serving chair of Coram's Fields, one of capital's oldest children's playgrounds, which in 1997 had been the venue for the launch of London Play (see Chapter Five). Apart from his association with play, as a former cabinet minister who was widely seen to have been a victim of Downing Street miscalculations over the Mayoral elections (and therefore owed a favour or two) Dobson was seen by the play sector as a potentially useful ally: a parliamentary heavyweight with connections at the heart of government.

For some years after he made it, it seemed that Chris Smith's Lottery pledge would be a red herring in the story of UK play policy, allowing the government to avoid the key issue of its own role in leading the planning and funding of play opportunities while nevertheless seeming to be acting as it had promised. After a long delay, his successor Tessa Jowell declined to comment on CPC's calls for a national play strategy, but instead announced a national play review – to be chaired by Frank Dobson – to advise the government and NOF on the best way to spend £200 million of lottery funding. This was good news; there had been a worry that the election pledge would be quietly forgotten and, given the resounding silence about our call for a government play strategy, we had to be glad that at least this opportunity appeared to be materialising. Some of us on the CPC had misgivings, however. Our recommendations had not been for Lottery funding, which is by nature short-term; one of the findings of *Making the case for play* had been that there was a surfeit of 'start-up' funding and pilot projects but a dearth of sustainable long-term investment. Would this not just be more of the same?

Doubts held in abeyance, CPC nevertheless agreed for our director Tim Gill to be seconded into the government to work with DCMS officials on the research and consultation phases of the review and to draft its report. Once inside Whitehall, Tim quickly confirmed that the report was 'the only game in town' as far as play policy was concerned and that, as a sector, we should drop the calls for a government play strategy, at least for now. Instead, he recommended seizing the opportunity represented by the promised NOF funding to build on the Better Play programme and using the Best Play outcomes framework to show what could be achieved with a much larger programme of ringfenced money for play.

The report of the Play Review, *Getting serious about play* (DCMS, 2003), was published after a wideranging national consultation that

CPC helped to facilitate. It made a number of recommendations to NOF and the government, essentially 'to improve and create thousands of spaces where children and young people can play freely and in safety'. It built on the Best Play approach to good provision, but used simpler, jargon-free language: one of the straight-talking Dobson's strengths.

Most of the Dobson Review's recommendations, drawn as they were from the sector's own suggestions, were uncontroversial. No one could argue, for example with advice that 'funding should be focused on areas and groups with the poorest access to good quality play opportunities' or the 'major emphasis on the inclusion of disabled children and young people'. There was less unanimity, though, with the proposed design of the programme's funding allocations. The report recommended that 'the bulk of the NOF funding – around 80 per cent – should support exemplary projects that follow and promote best practice' and that 'NOF should make a provisional allocation [of these] main funds to unitary and lower tier local authority areas on a basis that reflects the level of child poverty'. The remaining 20%, it said, should be used to promote innovation, aiming to find new approaches to play provision that might have lessons for the sector as a whole.

As a voluntary sector alliance that had only recently opened its membership to local authorities, there were some misgivings within CPC about local councils having such a dominant role. Local play associations and direct service providers in the charitable sector often experienced unequal and frustrating relationships with their local authorities, in which the overused term 'partnership' belied the imbalance. *Making the case for play* had now collated evidence, to boot, that many of them considered children's play a low priority and afforded its provision little or no strategic leadership. Against these concerns, the review had needed to consider that, whatever the variance in commitment to play from one authority to the next, local government was still the predominant provider. The voluntary sector in general, and in children's play in particular, simply did not have the reach to offer a consistent delivery chain for a national funding programme that aimed to cover every area of the country. The Play Review sought to address these worries by recommending that: 'the local authority or a local partnership should be responsible for drawing up proposals [...] prepared in partnership with other local agencies, children and young people and local communities'. It argued also that ringfenced funding should act as an incentive to local councils to raise their game on play, proposing that: 'NOF, the Government and local agencies should work together to ensure that all areas [...] have the necessary support to prepare sound, high-quality proposals and to implement them'.

In his foreword to the review, Frank Dobson, recognising the short-term nature of lottery funding and the long-term nature of the problem at hand, said: 'though it is not Government policy, I believe that a commitment to continue lottery funding of play facilities for the next decade would be a great step forward for children's play and also a sensible and popular use of lottery funds'. At the review's launch he took this recommendation a prescient step further, noting that, 'in a country where we have an Arts Council and a Sport England, distributing millions each year, is it not time that we also had a Play England?'

At the end of the Play Review's executive summary was printed – in a smaller font, as though added as an afterthought (which it probably was) – the disarming caveat: 'as part of its proposed reorganisation of the National Lottery funding arrangements, the Government is minded to abolish NOF as a separate entity'. Whatever the reservations that some in the sector may have had about the Play Review's proposals for a Lottery programme channelling most of its funding through local authorities, these were to quickly pale in significance compared to the dawning implication of these words.

The controversy over NOF's remit to develop programmes according to broad directions from ministers had caused the government to rethink its policy on Lottery funding. As a result, legislation was being prepared to merge NOF with the Community Fund to create one large distributor for charitable causes. This was to be known as the Big Lottery Fund (BIG) and, although the Dobson Review's footnote continued that: 'all our recommendations about the priorities and functions of NOF should apply to its successor', anyone who had followed the arguments about Lottery funding and government policy knew that this was a contradiction in terms. The reason for the government wanting to abolish NOF was precisely *because* it had come in for such criticism for setting its priorities in the first place; a departure from the 'additionality' principle of the independence of Lottery funding (Campbell, 2004) and its role in meeting needs not covered by statutory services.

There followed a period of huge uncertainty. The government had commissioned a review to advise it and a specific Lottery distributor on how to deliver a programme that had been announced by a government minister as an election pledge. Now it was about to dismantle that distributor on the basis that it no longer wanted to give such specific directions on how Lottery funding should be spent. Whatever Dobson recommended, it seemed his review might now have been in vain. Having introduced a seductive diversion to the play movement's main policy case – a national government play strategy – Chris Smith's pledge of Lottery funding now looked like it was backfiring even on itself.

At this juncture, it seemed clear to some of us at CPC that we would need to both raise the political stakes and to take the fullest possible advantage of our close links to NOF and the government. As an award partner for NOF's Better Play Programme and the leading advocate for the commitment made by Chris Smith – as well as the agency that had most supported Frank Dobson's review – we believed we were in as good a position as we could be to exert some influence. NOF's Chief Executive, Stephen Dunmore, was on the record as regarding Better Play as an unqualified success. We also knew that Frank Dobson and the government team at DCMS had a high regard for our director, Tim Gill, for his work on the Play Review and for his measured leadership of the sector.

There was a fine judgment to be made here. Being regarded by the government as an agency it could trust to do business with – a 'safe pair of hands' – counts for little if the policy objectives that one is seeking to progress fail to materialise. As it gradually became clear that the government's position was to welcome the Dobson proposals but to no longer ringfence any Lottery funding to implement them, we needed to remind ourselves what the first part of the term 'critical friend' actually meant.

The subsequent campaign to pressurise the government to honour its pledge of a £200 million Lottery programme for play would eventually have the desired effect, but not on its direct target. The government's full response to the Play Review, nearly four years after Chris Smith's election promise of 2001, was contained in a letter from Tessa Jowell (2005a) to Frank Dobson. Welcoming the review and accepting its proposals in full, the Secretary of State nevertheless confirmed that it was no longer government policy to direct Lottery funding to specific causes. Although she 'fully expected the lottery to take forward the review's recommendations' and 'spend £200 million on new and improved play opportunities', there would be no ringfenced money and no directions from the government to run a children's play programme. In the finest tradition of New Labour spin, the Secretary of State's letter to her former cabinet colleague was published under a government press release proclaiming: 'The government today reaffirmed its commitment to revitalising children's play areas'. In reality, this was no commitment at all. We knew that we would now have to apply pressure in a different direction (Mason, 2005).

NINE

'Lottery millions'

The Children's Play Initiative

CPC's role in first suggesting, then helping to design and deliver the Better Play Programme, had far-reaching consequences. Not least of these was the proximity it gave us to the senior team of a new, supersized funding body at a time when there was much to play for – and much to lose.

Unusually for the head of a large funder, New Opportunities Fund's (NOF) Chief Executive Stephen Dunmore had taken a personal interest and involved himself directly in some of Better Play's activities, particularly towards its latter stages. CPC's partnership with Barnardo's, one the country's oldest, largest and most respected children's charities, may well have helped to engender such a commitment – or perhaps it was simply that there is a 'feel-good factor' to good play projects that even CEOs find irresistible. Whatever the reason, Stephen Dunmore was a surprisingly frequent speaker at Better Play events and an engaging and interested contributor to the round of workshops that CPC and Barnardo's staged to finalise the programme and help to inform its conclusions. Prominent among these was the challenge of sustaining new projects within a wider policy and funding climate still largely disinterested in children's play.

In October 2004, there was still a good deal of uncertainty about the fate of the Play Review's recommendations and the prospects for a Lottery programme for play. Many in the sector wanted us to challenge what was being seen as a broken promise to children and continue to put pressure on the government to honour its election pledge. Having met with Tessa Jowell, we knew that her response to Frank Dobson, which had been a long time coming and was made in full consideration of the imminent changes to the laws governing Lottery funding, was final.

Crucially, Frank Dobson was no longer a minister. His report was in the way of recommendations to the government and to the funder, NOF. It was not government policy and could not, therefore, be construed as ministerial directions. We knew that the best chance for a national funding programme for play now lay in persuading not the government, but the newly created Lottery distributor, that this would be a popular, successful and worthwhile use of £200 million. As luck would have it, one of the first tasks in my new role as director of CPC that October was to host our Annual General Meeting (AGM), and it was with considerable gratitude to my predecessor Tim Gill – who had organised the agenda before he left – that this included introducing and chairing a question and answer session with our old friend Stephen Dunmore, now Chief Executive of the new Big Lottery Fund (BIG).

At this stage, BIG was not yet constituted as a new statutory funding body. This would require legislation that had yet to pass through Parliament. A simple passage was anticipated, however, and the merger of the two existing bodies – NOF and the Community Fund – had begun. The name, image and messages of the new body had been launched and it was busy developing the shape, themes and aims for this new era of Lottery funding. In short, BIG was looking for ideas for new programmes that could carry its stamp.

At the CPC AGM, Stephen Dunmore reiterated his view that the Better Play programme had been an 'absolute triumph' and was full of praise for our role in it. On the subject of the possibility of a much larger play programme he was understandably more cautious. After Tessa Jowell's public response to the Dobson Review, there was little that he could say other than to reiterate the government line that a range of different programmes would be expected to deliver children's play opportunities. He went further though, suggesting that not only BIG but also other Lottery distributors – such as the Heritage Lottery Fund, the Arts Council and Sport England – would be expected to contribute. When asked how he could be sure that this would happen – how different programmes for disparate causes managed by different funders could be made to adopt the Dobson recommendations, and particularly how the funder would ensure that a total of at least £200 million would be allocated in this way – he could only say that the details would have to be worked out. When we suggested that a much simpler solution, and one more likely to deliver the benefits that children needed, would be to develop a discreet programme along the lines of the Play Review's proposals, there was an unmistakable recognition between us that this was the way forward. He invited me to send him our ideas for how this could work and said he would be happy to meet and discuss them with us.

This was the opportunity that the play movement had been working towards for many years: a large enough sum of public money to improve or create new play provision across the whole country was now within reach. Frank Dobson's proposals had set out an authoritative vision for a national programme, which encompassed definitions of play and play provision that the sector could recognise as well as some broad criteria for how the funding could be allocated. It was clear that whatever proposal we put to Stephen Dunmore at BIG would need to build and elaborate on the Play Review.

Within the three weeks or so between CPC's AGM and my meeting with Stephen Dunmore, the national play conference in Sheffield, hosted by the Institute for Leisure and Amenities Management (ILAM), was held in Sheffield. One of the keynote speakers was BIG's head of policy, the former government advisor Philip Chamberlain. As CPC's new director, I had been asked to chair the event. This presented an opportunity to both discuss ideas with him privately in the conference margins, and to demonstrate to him the level of feeling in the sector about the importance of responding imaginatively to the Play Review. It was also a chance to clarify some of our thinking and to prepare BIG for what we were about to propose.

Still publicly holding the government line that funding for play would be distributed via a range of different programmes and different funders, Chamberlain then faced a difficult line of questioning from delegates – and others on the speaking panel – that challenged this idea as being unworkable. There was a real danger, said many delegates, that the multi-programme approach would water down the Dobson proposals and use incorrect definitions and inadequate criteria. The result, yet again, would be children's right to play being subsumed into other agendas. On a practical level, how would several different lottery distributors coordinate and collaborate sufficiently to monitor their diverse funded projects well enough to even know how much was being committed to play? The answer was unconvincing, but Chamberlain also gave us the strongest hint yet that BIG was ready to seriously consider a proposal to adopt the Dobson Review in full.

What BIG needed to be convinced of, Chamberlain told me away from the spotlight, was that a reliable 'delivery chain' could be put in place to ensure that a fully national play programme could be implemented in a way that was true to its aims. This was a reasonable question, and one that had also been exercising us at CPC. *Making the case for play* had only confirmed that in most parts of the country there was a limited understanding of what good play provision entails. Best Play, Quality in Play, the developing framework for recognised training and qualifications and the Better Play programme had all helped to achieve more recognition for playwork, but it was a long way from being universally adopted as the standard approach to working with children in out-of-school settings. The extent of staffed play provision, such as adventure playgrounds, was increasingly dwarfed by childcare and the new 'extended services' offering 'wrap-around care' (Curtis, 2004) for school-aged children through before- and after-school clubs. In some such settings playwork was finding a home as the standard for good practice, but in most places it was not.

Making the case for play had also demonstrated the dearth of planning for play and the lack of the necessary infrastructure to make it happen. Our call for a national strategy was as much to engender and develop a broader vision and a longer term approach to play provision as it was to inject dedicated funding into the sector. In other words, the reliable 'delivery chain' seen as so important by BIG to the viability of a new national play programme was also what our own research found to be missing. Play provision, as defined by Dobson and CPC, was a minority service. With 355 local authorities in the country, the challenge was how to ensure that the majority of them adopted the right policies, applied the right criteria, designed the right projects and employed the right staff to deliver projects that we would recognise.

On the train back from the ILAM conference in Sheffield, the CPC team took the chance to catch up on some reading. As well as studying *Getting serious about play* for the umpteenth time, looking for inspiration for our proposal to Stephen Dunmore, I also – with my former London Play hat on – had to proofread a draft copy of the Mayor of London's (2005) *Guide to preparing local play strategies*, which was being readied for publication in the New Year. A third document commanding my attention was a new evaluation of the Better Play programme. Reflecting on these various strategic play initiatives in the context of the one we were still trying to materialise, it dawned on us that the solution was right there in front of us.

We now felt confident that BIG shared with CPC the aim of creating a successful play programme. Its broad aims and objectives, everyone agreed, should be based on the Dobson Review. The conundrum was about how exactly to design it and what structures to establish to ensure that it would be both deliverable and true to these aims. Simply reiterating the Play Review recommendations would not suffice. We needed to show how they could be made to work.

In these deliberations, we had another consideration that may not have been quite so immediate to the funder. This was that CPC, looking ahead, had to also consider our real policy goal, which had never been a lottery programme, but a long-term commitment from government. Lottery funding was generally only for three years, while the Better Play programme had confirmed what *Making the case for play*, the Children's Fund and the Torkildsen report had already highlighted: the need for mainstream, sustained funding streams. We knew we would have to use whatever opportunities this programme presented to unarguably make the policy case to government for a national play strategy; such a chance would not come again for the foreseeable future.

The answer to all of this, we realised, was partly within the Play Review itself, partly within the design of the Better Play programme and partly within the strategic planning framework adopted by the London Mayor. Recognising that many, if not most, local authorities would have little experience of serious planning or innovative thinking about children's play, one of Dobson's recommendations was that 'NOF, the Government and [partnerships of] local agencies should work together to ensure that all areas [...] have the necessary support to prepare sound, high-quality proposals and to implement them'. This implied the need for three things: local play partnerships to involve the full range of relevant departments and agencies; longer-term whole area play strategies to underpin funding proposals and ensure their sustainability; and a specialist resource of support and guidance to those involved.

Fleshing out a proposal to BIG based on this broad structure gave rise to the inevitable question of what form the specialist support should take and who would provide it. Our good relationship with BIG in its NOF reincarnation and the widely regarded success of our Better Play partnership with Barnardo's – not to mention our leading role in supporting the Play Review – would inevitably put CPC in the frame for such a role. On the other hand, Frank Dobson, at the Review's launch, had made the suggestion that a new national body – a 'Play England' – should be established. Although this had been more in the way of an organisation to administer longer-term Lottery funding for play than a specific recommendation for this proposed programme, the idea had taken root.

There was a risk that our growing sense of a potentially huge opportunity to create a new infrastructure body for the play sector in England – whatever, and whoever, might run it – would distract us from the more immediate challenge of convincing Stephen Dunmore and colleagues that the programme was viable in principle. Furthermore, we sensed that any suggestion from us that our proposals were coloured by what could be construed as self-serving interests would be unproductive. We had to be careful not to get ahead of ourselves, and so agreed not to refer to any possible role for CPC at any stage of what we hoped would be an extensive dialogue.

The proposal that we put to Stephen Dunmore in November 2004 outlined a proposed national funding programme that adopted the broad recommendations of the Play Review in full and set out a plan to implement these in a number of different ways. It was a Dobson recommendation that local authorities should be the lead body in each area, invited to bid for a predetermined sum allocated to their area. To ensure that authorities applied the right definitions of play and play provision to their plans, we advocated that the award criteria be drawn from Best Play. We also proposed that there should be a requirement that a funding bid should only be submitted from each area once a crosscutting play strategy, developed by a multi-agency local play partnership including the voluntary sector, had been prepared and fully adopted by the authority. The all-important guidance and support to the 355 local authorities to be tasked with this challenge, we proposed, should be from nine regional support teams – based on the existing government structure of regional development agencies – with knowledge, skills and experience of play provision and play development. Finally, we proposed that there should be a discreet fund within the programme that should be open to applications from charities and community groups independently of local authorities and their play partnerships.

After receiving and discussing our proposals with us at some length, Stephen Dunmore invited us, as we had hoped, to engage in an extended dialogue with his team to develop the proposals into a detailed and costed plan. As yet, no commitment had been made – this would require a decision by BIG's board – but the prospects for the programme promised by Chris Smith in 2001 were looking better than they had for some time. As our discussions with BIG progressed, it became clear that the programme, as we had proposed it, was more likely to happen than not, but that they needed to have some assurances about the support structure that we had put forward. It made sense to them in principle, but in a sector with such a dearth of infrastructure they wanted to know who was likely to be ready and available to provide such a service. It would soon be time for CPC to show that our ambitions for the play sector could be matched by our capacity to support it.

In the first week of April 2006, the Children's Play Initiative was launched. The programme, said the announcement from BIG, was to:

- Create, improve and develop children and young people's free local play spaces and opportunities throughout England, according to need;
- Support innovation and new ways of providing for children's play;
- Create a support and development infrastructure to ensure local agencies have the resources and skills to achieve the first two aims;
- Promote the long-term strategic and sustainable provision for play as a free public service to children;

- Ensure that local authorities work with other local stakeholders to develop children's play strategies and plans;
- Ensure that good, inclusive and accessible children's play services and facilities are provided locally.

Although not yet government policy, as such, our ambition of securing strategic public sector commitments to support children's play was beginning to seem achievable. To fully realise it, though, the lottery millions would need to do more than create new projects.

TEN

'Dirt is good'

The Play England project

A small robotic figure about the size of a six-year-old child stands silently, without moving, in a darkened, dusty room. After some moments, dimly flickering lights start to appear behind its artificial eyes. Its rectangular, metallic head turns creakily to one side, then the other.

The robot starts to move forward with hesitant, jerky steps – as though nervous, or perhaps rusty. It slowly emerges, blinking, on to the patio of a domestic suburban garden. It stops, dazzled by the sunshine and unsure of the other elements too. It looks around at its leafy surroundings and hesitates again.

It walks towards the garden, even slower than before. As its robotic foot makes contact with the grass it stops suddenly and looks warily skywards. There is a sound of thunder. Raindrops begin to splash off its hard surfaces.

Alarmed, the robot looks down at its automated feet as the earth beneath them softens under the deluge. Except that it's automated, metallic limbs have now turned to flesh and blood. It is a human boy, now exploring, for the first time, the sensation of mud between his toes.

The boy squeals with delight and performs a spontaneous, muddy dance for no one but himself, before raising his arms skyward, arching his head back to feel the rain on his face, and laughs, long, loudly and without inhibition.

Dirt is good: all children have the right to play.

(TV and cinema commercial to promote Playday 2006)

Whatever the rationale within government thinking that would eventually lead to a serious commitment to children's play, there can be no question that the campaigning activity of Play England, made possible by some of the Lottery millions awarded to CPC for its key role in the Children's Play Initiative, had a big influence.

In 2005, the Big Lottery Fund (BIG) was still a new organisation, formed by a forced merger of two other bodies (Shifrin, 2003) with considerable upheaval. The proposal on its desk for a new £200 million funding programme for children's play would, if adopted, become its first large strategic programme. There was a lot at stake, not just for the play sector. A decision was made early in BIG's deliberations that, if the play programme was to go ahead, the £200 million pledged by Labour would be divided proportionately between its programme boards for each of the four home nations. This in itself seemed to confirm that the funder saw the policy implications of what we were proposing: children's play being within the remit of the powers variously devolved to the administrations of Scotland, Wales and Northern Ireland. This meant that influence on the funding decisions for those three nations was now in the hands of our colleagues at Play Scotland, Play Wales and Playboard Northern Ireland, leaving CPC, as it evolved into Play England, to focus on the £155 million funding programme for England.

To give our plans the green light, BIG's England committee would need to be convinced that the programme could deliver on its aims. The proposal to require local authorities to submit not just grant applications, but crosscutting area-wide strategies, would be controversial. Some local authorities would resent being told by a non-elected organisation what it should have strategies for and how to develop them. Putting significant resources into setting up a national support structure would also be a decision that could leave BIG open to criticism from those who believed that a larger portion of public funding should go to frontline services.

Against these reservations, we encouraged our advocates at BIG to argue that a programme designed not to fund projects and services for three years, but to effect a sea change in the planning and support structures that could grow and develop them into the future - in an area widely recognised as needing such an injection - was just the sort of bold, strategic initiative that the new funder should embrace, in keeping with its aim to be seen as the 'intelligent funder'.[1] A key to winning this argument would be the confidence it felt it could place in its chosen partner. We had begun to receive the impression that BIG was not seriously considering other organisations for the support role, but that they quite reasonably had concerns about CPC's capacity.

CPC was not a registered charity in its own right, or indeed any other kind of constituted body. Although it nominally held a small government contract and received some modest grants from one or two charitable trusts, in reality it was our host or parent body, National Children's Bureau (NCB), that was legally responsible for our work, employing all our staff and receiving and accounting for all our finances. CPC had an executive committee comprised of members elected by the full council, but the term was misleading, suggesting a formal responsibility that they did not have. Being essentially an alliance of other organisations, this arrangement with NCB suited CPC members well, allowing them to be involved in the formulation of joint policy positions and work programmes to promote them, while avoiding the responsibility of becoming trustees of another organisation. There were also cost efficiency benefits to sharing premises and other core functions with other councils and alliances under the NCB umbrella, and the considerable advantage of being part of a highly influential national children's charity with strong links to government. Now, however, there was an opportunity for the play movement to achieve an important milestone. The time seemed right to establish an independent national play charity. The Play England project was conceived.

We proposed to BIG that we should conceive Play England as a project in its own right. We were not going to simply put in place a structure to deliver a time-limited funding programme; we wanted to create a national body that, as well as supporting the Lottery programme for local play partnerships, would have its own broader aims: establishing itself as an independent charity, raising the profile of play, increasing awareness of the benefits and barriers

---

[1] The term 'intelligent funder' would become a well-used phrase in BIG's publicity materials (BIG, 2009) but was first used at its England Funding Committee meeting in 2007 in reference to the Children's Play Initiative.

to play opportunities and, crucially, developing the case for play policy with national as well as local government. Somewhat to our surprise, BIG agreed, and rather than awarding us a contract as an award partner, CPC was invited to submit a grant application with a deadline of Christmas 2005 to the brand new Children's Play Initiative (BIG, 2005), which would now have three strands: the Children's Play Programme, for local play partnerships; the Playful Ideas programme, for innovative projects from the voluntary sector; and a third for infrastructure capacity building: growing the new Play England. The final piece of the jigsaw in place, we submitted our bid on Christmas Eve 2005, and in February 2006 CPC was awarded £15 million over five years for 'the Play England Project'. The most immediate task in this rapidly dawning new era for CPC, after getting a nationwide recruitment programme underway, was to draft guidance for local play partnerships on the production of the play strategies that would be a required part of their applications for funding from the main programme. BIG needed this to be ready and printed by the end of March so that it could be dispatched along with the rest of the programme materials. Fortunately, we had one that we had prepared earlier!

The Mayor's (2005) *Guide to preparing local play strategies* was of course set within the specific context of London. Nevertheless, after consulting with an advisory group set up for the purpose and listening to feedback from the London boroughs that had begun to work with the guidance, it was clear that most of the principles, processes and steps set out in the Mayor's guide would translate comfortably into national guidance for unitary and second-tier authorities. We sought permission from the Mayor's office to borrow liberally from his document, and *Planning for play: Guidance on the development and implementation of a local play strategy* (Voce, 2006) was published in April as a key part of the programme guidance.

CPC was, by then, already beginning its transformation: ramping up our role of supporting local authorities to develop their play strategies as the basis for receiving Lottery funding under the main programme. Our BIG grant was wide-ranging, giving us the capacity for the campaigning and influencing activity that we needed to make the case for government policy. However, with 355 unitary and district municipalities each required to research, prioritise, plan and consult on their strategies (many of them, we knew, from a very low starting point), we had our work cut out to first make sure that the Lottery funding was spent effectively. Supporting local authorities via our nine regional teams was the main focus of our efforts in those early days of the transition and expansion from CPC into Play England. With the pressures of keeping a big funding programme on track in all of the 355 local authorities in the country, this was vital and challenging work.

Nevertheless, for all the big changes that the Lottery grant had brought, we had not lost sight of our longer-term goals. We were keenly aware that whatever commitments were made in their play strategies, three years' funding for local authorities would not be enough on its own to make play provision the long-term priority we knew it needed to be. Whatever some of our colleagues at NCB thought, a national government play strategy was no less of an objective after the Lottery programme had been secured than it was before. To achieve it we needed to broaden the alliance for play policy to include advocates and campaigners outside the play movement, and to amplify our messages to the public.

The years 2006-7 saw us undertake a wide array of influencing and campaigning activities, as our Lottery grant allocations for policy, research and communications bore some rich fruit. The 'Dirt is good' campaign with Persil was perhaps the highest profile of these, with the robot commercial shown on national television and cinema screens for a period of three to four weeks in July and August 2006, when the high-level campaign included pull-out centrespreads about children's right to play in the biggest selling tabloid newspapers. This unprecedented exposure for our cause culminated on Playday (2 August), when an estimated 1 million children attended free play events nationwide and our research findings – that 72% of children in the UK would prefer to play outside more often than they do – received serious news coverage on all the major channels.

As important as raising public awareness about children's right to play, was presenting the policy case for government action from some new and different platforms in ways that we knew – or hoped – would attract serious interest from policymakers. Demos was an influential, cross-party think tank with a track record of producing challenging reports and pamphlets on issues that resonated with the play movement, such as the potential threats (as well as the opportunities) posed by the 'childcare revolution' (Wilkinson, 2001) and how to create a more personal, liveable public realm (Bentley, 2003). When the most senior minister with responsibility for play, Culture Secretary Tessa Jowell (2005b), joined this debate with her own Demos essay suggesting that 'street safety is influenced not just by lighting and police patrols, but also by how well used a street turns out to be; on the flow of people walking through it', it seemed like a perfect opportunity to try to move children's play to the centre of the debate about our relationship with public space.

Seen and heard: Reclaiming the public realm with children and young people (Beunderman et al, 2007), was almost not published when Demos's policy of not including sponsors' branding on its imprint clashed with BIG's requirement that all publications funded by its grant should bear its logo. Thankfully, our communications team resolved the issue and the pamphlet was launched early in 2007, its potential influence vividly illustrated when eminent architect Lord Rogers joined Children's Minister Beverley Hughes at its launch event in the Young Vic theatre. The authors' provocative recommendation that an 'antisocial behaviour' hotline should be established – not for irate citizens to report the misbehaviour of 'hoodies' but for young people themselves to log incidents of being harassed in their play by inhospitable adults – raised many eyebrows and received controversial news coverage, but the overwhelming response, not least from government figures, was positive. The call for 'closer inter-departmental, inter-agency and cross-sectoral working' for a 'public realm that is understood as a shared resource' for all generations, with 'playable space, and playful streets […] the normative vision guiding the ambitions for urban renaissance and sustainable communities' (Beunderman et al, 2007)was no longer a cry in the wilderness or even simply a requirement for local authorities to receive lottery funding. Children's stake in public space as their rightful place to play was rising to the top of the public policy agenda.

Nevertheless, in spite of this growing interest in an emergent debate about children, young people and public space, the government's official line on play policy during the early years of the Children's Play Initiative (2006–7) remained obdurately laissez-faire. A working group of civil servants from a range of departments and various play sector 'experts' hosted by DCMS produced a document, *Time for play* (DCMS, 2006), which spoke of an 'on-going commitment to children's play' but proposed nothing in the way new policy, instead seeming to take credit for the work now being done with the Lottery funding by Play England and the local play partnerships without addressing the big question of how this would be sustained after the end of the initiative in 2010–11. In typically straight-talking fashion, Frank Dobson – as keenly aware as anyone of the need for a longer-term commitment than Lottery funding to secure the changes proposed in his review – dismissed *Time for play* as 'not worth the paper it's written on' (Dobson, 2006).

Having echoed Dobson's sentiments (and quoted his words) in the editorial of *Play Today*, our news and articles periodical, it was with some trepidation that I met with David Lammy, the Culture Minister who had commissioned the *Time for play* report, in the spring of 2007. Lammy had flatly told one of our play conferences earlier that year that a national play strategy was 'not going to happen', and it seemed to me that our continued campaign to the contrary – made possible by funding that, in all honesty, would not have been available had his party not promised it – might be something of an irritant. I couldn't have been more wrong. Lammy had called the meeting after reading our Demos report and began by saying that *Seen and heard* was one of the most inspiring policy reports he had read for some time, and that our criticism of his department's own bland document was in fact helpful, better enabling him to make the case for a more proactive government response with his fellow ministers. He acknowledged that there were considerable limits to what his department could do, but that he could see the need for a collaborative approach across different government policy areas. The most tangible outcome of our meeting was his think piece published by left-of-centre think tank, Compass, echoing the Demos report:

> For years, children were expected to be 'seen and not heard'. In urban planning we need them to be both; because for children to have the best chance to be happy, healthy and to prosper, they need to have a real stake in the common spaces of their neighbourhoods. Among the hustle and bustle of our modern towns and cities we need to engender local 'village' communities, where children are looked after in the widest sense. This

must start with somewhere for our children – all our children – to play. (Lammy, 2007)

While falling short of specific policy proposals, this was the most fulsome statement yet made by a serving minister on the question of children's play, not as medium for their improved 'learning outcomes' in school or childcare, but as a key to their right to a proper stake in the spaces and places of the public realm.

The optimism engendered by Lammy's piece for Compass was not simply a result of its content but of the knowledge we now had about conversations he was having, as the minister with responsibility for play, with other ministers. The former chair of CPC, Helen Goodman, was now a junior minister and agreed to chair a new All Party Parliamentary Group on Children's Play, which helped to promote these talks and to win support for a serious policy initiative. Like David Lammy, Helen was also connected with Compass, leading a review for the think tank about the 'commercialisation of childhood' (Williams, 2006), which culminated in a 'Charter' supported by the National Union of Teachers (NUT, 2007), the country's largest teachers' union. The NUT had, itself, already called for 'local authorities to develop play policies in partnership with schools and young people to establish a strategic and practical framework for play provision throughout children's services', further evidence of the growing support for a strategic government play policy.

The range and scale of the influences adding their weight to our cause was growing, as was the level of interest now being expressed by ministers. After nearly 40 years, Lady Allen's vision of playable community spaces supported by specific public policy – our own ambitions for a national government play strategy – seemed tantalisingly within reach.

ELEVEN

'The best place in the world'

The Play Strategy for England

On a sunny south London morning in March 2008, on a leftover piece of urban land – a brownfield site in the planning jargon, but one long since colonised by playing children – there is an unusual spectacle.

Four middle-aged men in suits and ties are swinging, two of them in tandem, in long, high arcs. Clinging for all they were worth to thick, sturdy lengths of rope suspended from homemade, brightly painted wooden structures made from old telegraph poles and assorted planks of scrap wood, the men appear tentative at first, clumsy and ungainly in their buttoned up shirts, shiny shoes and politician manners. It seems certain that one or more of them will lose his grip; crashing his bones, dignity, and very likely his career into the rubble and nettles below. There are no safety surfaces here.

Gradually, though, the men's confidence visibly increases as they seem to recall long-forgotten skills. Nervous pleasure turns to something close to unrestrained glee; they begin to enjoy themselves. Concentrated on the physical immediacy and real challenge of these monster swings, they become lost in the moment. For a few minutes these serious, powerful men forget how important they are and what they might look like in the newspapers the next day. They remember how to play.

More grown-up looking people, about 30 of them, equally unsuitably attired for the ramshackle environment in which they find themselves, take photographs and videos, make notes on clipboards, look anxiously at watches, speak over-excitedly on mobile phones or just look on, nervously. A group of children marched in for the occasion from a nearby primary school wait on the periphery looking bored. Still the men play on their swings, laughing now and egging each other on until, anxiously, one of the onlookers gesticulates that they should stop. It is time to get on with the business of the day.

Ed Balls, Secretary of State for Children, Schools and Families, was perhaps to later regret his few minutes of fun at Slade Gardens Adventure Playground. One of the videos of he and Andy Burnham, the Culture Secretary, swinging together from the same dual swing structure, was widely shown on TV news reports, mainly as the lighthearted item to sign off a bulletin before the weather forecast. The item attracted a degree of ridicule, not just from opponents but also from the political commentariat in general. *The Daily Telegraph* said the pair looked 'more like a pair of overgrown schoolboys than two of the most powerful men in the country' (Malkin, 2008). Comedians had fun with it too; the long-running satirical panel show, *Have I Got News For You*, famed for its merciless lampooning of political pomp and spin, featured the clip on primetime BBC television later that week. Balls's and Burnham's stunt was likened unkindly to the baseball-capped, rollercoasting antics that had so backfired on the Conservative leader William Hague some years earlier, which was seen by some to have undermined his projection as a future Prime Minister.

Some might say that politicians, especially when the cameras are rolling (and in the modern era, when aren't they?), should stick to what they are good at, or at least what is expected of them. The civil servants, special advisers and media managers at Slade Gardens that morning had not expected their ministers to quite so indulge themselves. Too like a grisly scene from another political satire, *The Thick of It*, in which politicians' attempts at the common touch only ever embarrass everyone concerned and incur the wrath of the spin doctors, this clearly was not a photo op they had planned; hence the strained, nervous laughter. The unintended irony – at this moment of all moments – of describing childlike behaviour in the pejorative will have passed by most of *The Daily Telegraph*'s readers, but on this occasion the mockery seemed a little unfair. Beneath the dos and don'ts of ministerial image management, here were two men simply unable to resist the opportunity to play.

Ed Balls understood the value of places like Slade Gardens – real adventure playgrounds that afford children opportunities worthy of the name – and how important they must be to children, especially those living in the crowded inner-city neighbourhoods where most children have no garden of their own and good space to play is hard to find. When he was finally persuaded to remember what he was there for and, somewhat shambolically, to dismount his swing, it was to unveil the first ever national government Play Strategy (DCSF/ DCMS, 2008b).

The government was committed to changing a culture, Balls told the waiting reporters, in which 'it seems children spend less time playing outside than they would like and less than their parents did as children'. He cited CPC's evidence that '"as many as one in four children, aged eight to 10, have never played outside without an adult"' (BBC News, 2008) and said, in his foreword to the strategy consultation document, 'We want local authorities to give a high priority to supporting and promoting outdoor play – with play and public play space being seen as an essential characteristic of a healthy community' (DCSF/DCMS, 2008a). The proposed solution was a wide-ranging 12-year plan in three phases that aimed for 'all children and young people [to] be able to find places, near their homes, where they can play freely [...] meet their friends [and] feel confident and safe to play, both indoors and out [...] in a manner that is appropriate to their needs and interests' (DCSF/DCMS, 2008a). Ed Balls had announced the government's intentions to produce a play strategy in December 2007, (Voce, 2007), when it featured as a central part of his new Children's Plan. This was the government's renewed policy for integrated education, social care and health services that aimed to refresh its Every Child Matters framework of universal outcomes for children, with the even bolder aim to make England 'the best place in the world to grow up' (DCFS, 2007).

With the UK ranked that same year by UNICEF (2007) at the bottom of a league table of children's wellbeing indicators in developed nations, this was quite an ambition – and one which, the government was finally acknowledging, would require tackling questions not just about children's services and the effects of poverty but about how the wider public realm responded to children in general. Making

England a better place to play – let alone the best in the world – would obviously mean more and better public play provision, and there was to be close to £190 million over three years to build new playgrounds and play areas. It would also mean an approach to planning, spatial development and community engagement that specifically included children's perspectives not just as potential victims or villains of the peace, but as stakeholders and citizens with their own agency.

Children and young people's need for independent mobility, safer built and social environments, better access to open space, and services designed with their input and reflecting their culture would all need to be part of the vision and included in the plan. A prerequisite to achieving this culture change would be some underpinning knowledge and skills from play theory and playwork practice, delivered through national training and professional development for the full range of sectors involved in designing, planning, building and managing the public realm.

As I said for a *Guardian* comment piece at the time, (Voce, 2008) 'such steps will require cross-departmental cooperation at all levels of government. Amazingly, the Play Strategy takes on all these challenges'. Tim Gill, now forging a career as an independent writer on childhood issues, concurred that the strategy was putting 'real money into the vision that children should be seen and heard in their communities, not reared in captivity' (Gill, 2008a). The Play Strategy was, he said, 'sending a clear message that planning and transport policies have to take their needs more seriously'.

Not everyone welcomed the Play Strategy. Kevin Harris of Neighbourhood consultants Local Level said it 'seems to be about confining children to manicured, designated places, while making those designated places more imaginative [...] the agenda could be seen as a predetermined reinforcement of segregation' (O'Hara, 2008). There was also scepticism within the play movement about the capacity, or willingness, of some local authorities to fully embrace the Play Strategy agenda – concerns not alleviated by the balance of funding in the first phase. With the Playbuilder capital programme forming the major part of the contracts with local authorities, there were fears that they would spend all the money on 'new kit' without making any longer-term commitments to change their approach and make children's play a greater priority for their own plans.

In fact, these changes in approach by local authorities were integral to the wider aims of the Play Strategy (DCSF/DCMS 2008b), as was a growth, for the first time since their 1970s and 1980s peak, in the number of real adventure playgrounds. These ambitions were not deferred to the strategy's next phases, either, but integral to the concurrent Pathfinder programme whereby 30 local authorities – as well as their Playbuilder funding – would receive an additional £1 million to design and build a new staffed adventure playground and to begin work on the longer-term measures, conceived to raise the profile and importance of children's play within local policy and planning processes and across children's services, and to take the concept of local play strategies into the top tier of local government decision making. This was the vision we had worked for many years to develop and promote within policy circles: a government-backed framework for bringing together key people in local government planning, housing, police, parks, leisure and children's services so that common aims and understandings about children's play in the public realm could be made to underpin key policies and plans across a whole area, and ensure that funding priorities included making proper provision for it.

To facilitate this process of active, influential play partnerships in each county and urban authority, Play England was contracted by the DCSF to deliver a package to play partnerships that we called Play Shaper.[1] Beyond simply training what would be a quite senior grouping of professionals from the relevant different departments, Playshaper was constructed as a facilitated event designed to enable dialogue, discussion and agreed action for play in each respective area, as well as keeping the local authority's play strategy current and integrated within wider plans and strategies, such as its green space strategy, its children and young people's strategy and ultimately its overarching statutory community strategy.

In addition to the Playshaper events, the government also contracted us to produce guidance to local authorities. Called *Embedding the Play Strategy* (DCSF, 2010), this document was intended to:

---

[1] See www.playshaper.org.uk

1. Enable senior decision makers and strategic planners to identify how play and child-friendly public space contributes to achievement against a range of national indicators and local priorities, including the play indicator (NI199).
2. Help Directors of Children's Services, Directors of Public Health, Chief Planning Officers, Directors of Transport and other senior executives and strategic decision makers to understand their roles and responsibilities in improving these outcomes through implementation of the Play Strategy locally.
3. Guide Directors of Children's Services and commissioners in developing and adopting local play strategies, underpinned by a thorough needs analysis, which can feed into the Children and Young People's Plan (CYPP).
4. Assist Children's Trusts in meeting their obligations to work closely with their LSP to develop excellent facilities and opportunities for outdoor play and recreation, as described in statutory guidance for Children's Trusts.
5. Provide a framework for the strategic planning expected of pathfinder and playbuilder authorities [...] and for embedding and sustaining this investment.
6. Offer updated guidance to play partnerships within authorities on developing and reviewing their existing local play strategies and, where relevant, on working between top-tier, second tier and unitary authorities to coordinate planning and delivery of local provision within the area-wide strategic framework. (DCSF, 2010)

Government guidance can sometimes be viewed with a degree of scepticism, especially when it has no statutory basis, and it is true to say that not every local authority, especially the non-Labour ones, was falling over itself to fully embrace this agenda. However, the Playshaper events, which brought a much more personal touch to the programme, would result in many 'penny-dropping' moments, where hardened professionals came to realise the importance of play for children and how their role could make a difference, for better or worse.

More cynically, as long as local authorities were receiving central government funding – with the National Indicator for play offering the prospect of more – they were, if not happy, then at least compliant in adopting our (and now the government's) vision, which was that 'Local authorities will be expected to develop and embed top-tier strategic approaches to play that are fully linked to their wider strategic planning' (DCSF, 2010). According to *Embedding the Play Strategy*, the government wanted 'the investment to catalyse closer working across authorities, between children's services, planners and developers, highways officers and other professionals who shape, manage and supervise public space so that more child-friendly communities can be created, ending the "no ball games" culture'.

Building on the experience of the Mayor of London's original guidance and the BIG Children's Play Programme, which had

Figure 1: How the Play Strategy saw children's play provision within the local strategic planning framework

Source: DCSF (2010)

produced 350 local play strategies, the government guidance identified ten essential elements for a successful local play strategy:

1. **Cross-cutting:** top level commitments within the CYPP, Sustainable Community Strategy and Local Development Framework with links to open space, transport and housing.
2. **Strong leadership:** a lead officer with appropriate seniority and resources, supported by a play champion within the council or relevant cabinet.
3. **High-level support:** support for a cross-cutting, collaborative approach from the Director of Children's Services and the Chief Planning Officer.
4. **Sound basis:** based on a comprehensive play audit and needs assessment.
5. **Participative:** active participation of children and young people, parents and community members.
6. **Inclusive:** actively includes disabled children, children from minority ethnic communities, and children living with social or economic disadvantage.
7. **Commitment:** commitments are defined as SMART[2] objectives with a timetabled action plan.
8. **Resourced:** activities are resourced and there is a commitment to sustainability.
9. **Learning:** regular monitoring, evaluation and review.
10. **Knowledge and understanding:** input from play sector experts, including playworkers and third sector organisations supporting play. (DCSF, 2010)

In addition to the framework for local commissioning for play within Children's Trust arrangements, the Play Strategy aimed to also engage planning departments in the mission to create play-friendly neighbourhoods, with DCSF commissioning Play England to produce new guidance (Cole-Hamilton et al, 2009) in partnership with officials at the Department of Communities and Local Government as a forerunner to promised changes in national planning policy. Dwarfing all other Play Strategy commitments in

---

[2] SMART: specific, measurable, achievable, resourced and timed, a common acronym in management planning.

its first phase, however — in ambition of scale, if not imagination — was the Playbuilder programme to create or rebuild 3,500 play areas in less than three years.

TWELVE

'Playbuilders'

Breaking the mould of the public playground

In North London, less than half a mile away from the noise and pollution of the Archway roundabout on the ever-congested A1, some children are looking for refuge. Living on the sprawling social housing estates that sit uncomfortably close to this unceasing melee of traffic, commuters and employees of the various welfare agencies housed by the forbidding Archway Towers, they head for the idyllic Waterlow Park, situated halfway up the steeply inclining road that connects their own working class inner-city neighbourhood to the affluence of nearby Highgate.

Waterlow Park is one of the many historic parks and gardens that set London apart from many other large capital cities. Situated close to the expanses of Hampstead Heath and tucked away between the imposing arts centre of Lauderdale House on one side, and the famous Highgate Cemetery on the other, it is less well frequented than many and has a peaceful, secluded charm.

To these children from the Archway estate this place is – as Sydney Waterlow described when bequeathing it to the London County Council in 1889[1] – a 'garden for the gardenless': somewhere spacious and green, where they can play in relative freedom with their friends, away from the traffic.

There is an old children's playground in Waterlow Park, next to the duck pond. Curiously, given that the park is located on a steep natural hill, the playground is flat and devoid of vegetation, with an

---

[1]   See: www.waterlowpark.org.uk/history

asphalt floor except beneath the various pieces of standardised equipment, where there is a synthetic rubber-like surface designed to reduce the risk of harm in the unlikely event that children might fall from it. The equipment comprises two rows of three swings each, one for toddlers. There is a roundabout, a climbing frame and a seesaw, each made primarily of wrought iron painted in primary colours, now faded and peeling. It is typical of the many thousands of playgrounds built in Britain during the middle part of the 20th century and occasionally renewed to more or less the same template ever since. These children from Archway have long since stopped using it, discovering very quickly that there was more fun to be had simply exploring the undulations of the park or making up their own games in and out of its many wooded areas or around its ponds.

Today, however, there is something new. The park has been designated for investment from Camden Council's allocation from the Playbuilder programme and the results of the work are ready to enjoy. The local children know about it because one of the stipulations of the programme was that they should be asked what they would like to see done with the money. 'Something big to climb on, but also to play games on', they said, 'and a much bigger swing: a rope swing'.

If you ask children open questions about what they would like for a play area, the answers can be impressive but unachievable; 'a swimming pool with fountains and dolphins and massive TV screens all around for kids to watch while they sunbathe' was one famous request. But given some parameters they are not especially demanding, and what these children wanted in Waterlow Park was not prohibitively expensive either to build or to maintain. As well as climbing and swinging, they wanted a place that was both identifiably for play, but also integrated within the overall park rather than fenced off from it. They did not want their play to be limited to the playground, or the equipment to be out of sight behind the pond and its willow trees, like the old one.

One of the most striking things about the new Waterlow Park play area is that it is not a clearly defined space. There are a number of installations, scattered over a fairly small part of the park, but they are not fenced in; there is no boundary. Another is that some of the basic concepts have been re-interpreted.

The new climbing frame is a large, freeform, organic structure of irregular lines, angles and spaces constructed from natural, treated logs and rope. No two sections are identical; climbing it requires some concentration and it lends itself to games. The swing is a single tyre suspended from an impressive, solid, semi-arched wooden structure. It has a long arc and can be mounted from either of two raised mounds. The mounds themselves are protected from erosion by rubber matting that allows the grass to grow while mitigating wear and tear and providing purchase for small feet in wet weather.

There are other, smaller additions: a carved totem pole, a rotating balancing beam, some boulders and wooden blocks to negotiate in the way of a mini assault course. Each of these items blends with the overall landscape, which uses the trees, bushes, grass and natural topography of the park as design features that afford more play value while also enabling the space to seem and feel integral to, rather than separate from, the park as a whole. The location of the equipment places the play area at the heart of the whole space, halfway down and in the centre of the grassy hill that falls away to the boundary with Highgate Cemetery. Notwithstanding the many trees, it is visible from all over the park.

The children from Archway love it and spend all day there, sometimes on the equipment but just as often playing throughout the surrounding area and the rest of the park, with its many wooded invitations to adventure. Visiting families picnic all around the undefined play area, where children play as and when they like without needing to be 'taken to the playground', which is now barely used at all.

To be accurate, the document launched by Ed Balls in March 2008 was not the final Play Strategy but a publication called *Fair play: A consultation on the play strategy* (DCSF/DCMS 2008a) in which the government was 'seeking to promote discussion about how we could all [...] build a society with more and better opportunities for all children to play'. But, with the £225 million announced in the House of Commons now increased to £235 million (as a small contribution to the fiscal stimulus that was part of the government's response to the unfolding financial crisis) and allocated as predominantly capital expenditure for the three-year period beginning just a couple of weeks later in April 2008, the essence of the strategy's first phase – a building programme for new and renovated playgrounds – was, in fact, already decided. This first major phase of the Play Strategy was christened the Playbuilder Programme. The 155 top-tier and unitary local authorities of England were tasked with building or renewing at least 3,500 play areas between them between April 2008 and March 2011. Subject to their plans being approved by the department, they would each have approximately £1 million of central government funding to do so.

Because it was to deliver the most immediate and tangible outcome – the new play areas where they were most needed – Playbuilder was to become the most well-known and recognisable part of the strategy. Along with the decision – like the Big Lottery Fund's – to allocate the vast majority of the money to local authorities, it was also to prove the most controversial within the play movement. Many would have preferred to see less funding for municipal, fixed equipment playgrounds, however reconceived, and more for voluntary sector playwork projects like adventure playgrounds.

Playbuilder was an ambitious programme. Conceiving, planning and procuring 3,500 playgrounds over a period considerably less than three years – once the arrangements, contracts and protocols for it had been put in place for 155 local authorities – was a big challenge by any standards. From Play England's perspective, it came with some equally big risks; not just for the strategy, but also for our own reputation. We had not lobbied for funding for fixed equipment playgrounds, believing them to be, more often than not, part of the problem. We shared a widespread view – not always but often fully justified by what was available on the ground – that, in reducing the concept of children's play space to some serviceable but soulless equipment seemingly designed more for exercise than play, public playgrounds were selling children short. Further, in perpetuating the idea that children's play is dependent on dedicated areas – usually fenced off from the wider public space where they are situated – the standard municipal playground was, in many eyes, emblematic of the constraints on children rather than the type of provision that would help to liberate them.

A proliferation of synthetic safety surfacing since the 1980s had also exacerbated the feeling that local authority procurement practices for play provision tended to err on the side of health and safety at the expense of play value. The practice of covering playgrounds with rubber or its equivalent had inspired many a debate (Ball, 2015) about whether such surfaces even mitigated against serious injuries, or actually made them more likely, as children are lured into a false sense of security. There were questions, too, about whether these surfaces were indeed safer in the event of a heavy fall, or amplified the trauma by rebounding the shock of impact back up through the body. Whatever their impact absorbing properties, there was no doubt that synthetic safety surfaces absorbed large parts of often meagre local authority play budgets and tended to perpetuate the idea that the design of children's playgrounds started with a catalogue.

There were some notable exceptions, where a new type of playground was emerging, influenced by the work of people like Helle Nebelong from Denmark and Sue Gutteridge from Stirling in Scotland. Championed by the likes of Spiegel (2011) and Gill (2013), a new aesthetic for public playgrounds was emerging, typically featuring landscaping and planted areas, bespoke woodwork, water features and community art rather than the metal climbing frames and 'springy chickens' that had become the norm. Sometimes dismissed as a type of middle-class gentrification of playgrounds – mainly by the manufacturers of the 'brightly painted ironmongery' that were its *bête noire* – this approach simply applies the same design principles to a play area as one would expect for any other public space that needs to be well-loved, only with extra consideration of the particular needs of children and their play.

This approach is described by Nebelong (2004) as beginning with the 'essential genius loci, the spirit of the place; in other words the qualities and the atmosphere already present' and then creating features that appeal to children's senses without patronising them. 'I think it is an adult idea', she says, 'created by misunderstanding, that everything to do with children must be openly amusing and painted in bright colours [...] Nature's own colours are perfect for the playground, maybe spiced up here and there with a few artistic colour splashes'. In this approach, standardised equipment is also a mistake: 'dangerous', says Nebelong (2004), because 'when the distance between all the rungs in a climbing net or a ladder is exactly the same, the child has no need to concentrate on where he puts his feet [...] play becomes simplified and the child does not have to worry about his movements. This lesson cannot be carried over to all the knobbly and asymmetrical forms with which one is confronted throughout life'. Examples of the approach advocated by Nebelong and others were very much the exception rather than the rule and by 2008 it seemed that, for all the advances in what was understood to constitute a good play environment – elemental play, loose parts, wild areas, opportunities for self-build and so on – that had been made by playwork in the UK, the more standard template for public playgrounds was as limited and limiting as ever.

Although an equally constraining factor on procurement practices was the limited revenue budgets for unstaffed play services that made low maintenance costs a key consideration in any tender, there was nevertheless a growing consensus (Play Safety Forum, 2002) that risk aversion – not of harm to children so much as public opprobrium or legal damages should the local authority be held responsible for it – was the main culprit. Questions of risk and safety in children's play provision had been the subject of some considerable focus by the Children's Play Council since we had assumed the role, under our government contract, of convening the Play Safety Forum (PSF): 'a grouping of national agencies involved in play safety'[2] to develop a consensus approach to the thorny issue and support providers in adopting it.

The PSF (2002) had produced a position statement aiming to address the problem of 'how safety is being addressed in children's play provision [...] and its consequences for their development'. Citing the research of David Ball, Professor of Risk Management at Middlesex University, the statement says, 'this approach ignores clear evidence that playing in play provision is a comparatively low risk activity for children. Of the two million or so childhood accident cases treated by hospitals each year, less than two per cent involve playground equipment'. While acknowledging the obvious (and legal) reality that 'play provision aims to manage the

---

[2] www.playengland.org.uk/resources/managing-risk-in-play-provision-a-position-statement.aspx

level of risk so that children are not exposed to unacceptable risks of death or serious injury', it then asserts that 'risk-taking is an essential feature of play provision', and, crucially, establishes that 'safety in play provision is not absolute and cannot be addressed in isolation [...] if it is not exciting and attractive to [children], then it will fail, no matter how safe'. This document had been well received by play service managers and others wanting to combat the risk averse culture (Gill, 2007) and see more imaginative designs and commissions for public play space. However, in spite of its endorsement by the statutory Health and Safety Executive, there was a good deal of anecdotal evidence that, in the main, a safety first approach and a preference for standardised manufactured equipment was still dominating the sector.

Play England's lottery funding had enabled us to invest quite substantially in developing resources that would support and promote better practice in play provision. After some informal discussions with key members of the Play Safety Forum we decided to commission a more extensive document on managing risk in play provision, which would expand on the position statement and provide an authoritative guide to the kind of risk benefit analysis that could assure providers that they were compliant with Health and Safety law, while allowing for the special nature of play provision and children's need to take risks (Ball et al, 2008).

Also, as part of our good practice promotion – funded by the BIG grant – Play England had commissioned a new design guide for unstaffed children's play areas that was intended to break the mould of the 'KFC playground'.[3] With much of the work on these two documents completed but not yet published at the time of the Play Strategy announcement, we saw the Playbuilder and Pathfinder programmes as an opportunity to have some new good practice principles not only promoted by the government but also immediately adopted and implemented as part of the single biggest investment in children's play the country had ever seen.

Design for play (Shackell et al, 2008), published jointly by Play England and the government, was 'intended to inform the creation of outdoor play space for years to come, that does justice

---

[3] KFC: Kit, Fence and Carpet, a term coined by Helen Woolley of the University of Sheffield, to denote the stereotypical municipal playground and its poor play value.

to children's endless capacity for adventure and imagination, their fundamental need for exercise and social interaction and, above all, to their innate sense of fun'. Just as importantly, it was 'also aimed at those responsible for the wider public realm', arguing that 'play space should be integrated sensitively into the wider design of the public realm'. The research informing *Design for play* had established that successful play spaces – by criteria consistent with current understandings about play – depended on ten principles, namely that they:

1. Are bespoke
2. Are well-located
3. Make use of natural elements
4. Provide a wide range of play experiences
5. Are accessible to both disabled and non-disabled children
6. Meet community needs
7. Allow children of different ages to play together
8. Build in opportunities to experience risk and challenge
9. Are sustainable and appropriately maintained
10. Allow for change and evolution. (Shackell et al, 2008)

The document expanded on each of these and set out some recommended processes. While, perhaps inevitably, not fully reflected in the design of every Playbuilder site, it soon became one of the most downloaded government guidance documents of all time and has unquestionably had a big influence on the shape and character of public play areas in England and beyond. In the event, this was just as well. Although not the priority of the play movement represented by Play England, the makeover for many of England's play areas was to be the only tangible legacy of the Play Strategy, which was soon to fall victim of much a bigger, global event and its political fallout.

THIRTEEN

'Everyday adventures?'

Austerity brings an end to play policy in England

To anyone able to accurately read the political runes, the premature end of the Play Strategy after only two of its planned 12 years could have been foretold even before it was launched in 2008. However, contrary to appearances since 2010, the prospects for a serious Conservative government play policy, before the financial crash of 2007, had been surprisingly good.

On succeeding Tim Gill as director of the Children's Play Council in 2004, I was granted a meeting with the Conservative Shadow Chancellor, Oliver Letwin, whose comments about us on Radio 4 had been so dismissive. After a slightly tense introduction, he eventually acknowledged that his characterisation of us was ill-informed and promised he would do what he could to help sow the seeds for a more enlightened approach from his party, before cutting the meeting short to rush off and vote.

The Conservatives, in opposition, then had not had much to say about children's play until a letter appeared in *The Daily Telegraph* in September 2006 (Abbs et al, 2006). Earlier that year, former head teacher Sue Palmer (2006) had published a book about what she termed the 'epidemic of misery' in the children of affluent developed nations. Palmer examined the big statistical increases in the numbers of children and young people with mental health, behavioural and eating disorders, and the rising levels of pupils classified as having additional needs in school. She suggested that these modern childhood ailments were the result of human evolution not being able to keep up with the pace of technological advances that had so changed the way that we live. Simply, modern life – including the radical reduction in children's freedom to roam and to play – was, according to Palmer, making them unwell.

Over a hundred academics, writers and medical experts signed the *Telegraph* letter endorsing Sue Palmer's diagnosis. It called for a closer examination of the quality of children's lives, saying that they were increasingly tainted by overexposure to electronic entertainment, lack of play space and the emphasis on academic testing in schools. '[Children] still need what developing human beings have always needed', it said, including 'real (as opposed to junk) food, real play (as opposed to sedentary, screen-based entertainment), first-hand experience of the world they live in and regular interaction with the real-life significant adults in their lives'. *The Telegraph* is the broadsheet of choice for most Conservatives, and Britain's biggest selling broadsheet newspaper. When it launched a campaign the following day under he banner 'Hold on to Childhood', the party was quick to respond; David Willets, the Conservative education spokesman, was quoted as giving it his full support.

At Play England, meanwhile, our greatly increased capacity – which included substantial budgets for research, publications and national media activity – had enabled us to quickly build a much higher public profile than had been possible as CPC, and to develop some effective influencing activity (see Chapter Ten). For that year's national Playday – the first since Play England's launch – we had decided to promote the theme of outdoor play and the importance of children having access to green and natural environments. We commissioned a research review (Lester and Maudsley, 2006), which explored children's 'strong and deep-rooted sensitivity to the natural world' and its connection with play. It found that 'children play instinctively with natural elements' and that 'play is the process whereby children fulfil their drive to affiliate with nature'. 'There is substantial evidence', it said, 'that supports the wide-ranging values and benefits arising from children's play in natural settings', but also that 'extensive research indicates that opportunities for children to access and play freely in natural spaces are currently seriously compromised'.

Working with the BBC's long-running popular children's television programme *Newsround* and the market research company IPSOS Mori, our Playday campaign in 2006 also produced a survey – highlighted on all the main news channels and in the press – showing that 80% of children in the UK prefer playing outside when given the choice, but that their chances to do so were limited. The survey found that nearly three out of four of them (72%) would like to play out more often than they did, while 86% said that they preferred outdoor activities – including playing out with their friends, building dens and getting muddy – to playing computer games (Play England/IPSOS Mori, 2006)

While wanting to counter the popular misconception that children were hooked on electronic entertainments out of choice and prompt parents to give them more opportunities to be outside, our more strategic aim for this campaign was to engage policymakers to think more seriously about the erosion of children's access to the outside world and their freedom to play there. Our press release lay down this challenge:

> What children are telling us is that they want more opportunities to play out, in stimulating natural spaces where they can have fun, be with their friends and use their imagination. It is vital for both national and local governments to take this message on board if they are to meet the play needs of today's children and young people.

Soon after Playday and around the time of the *Telegraph* letter, we were invited to meet with David Willets, who told us he had been highly impressed by our Playday campaign and was highly sympathetic to the cause of promoting more outdoor natural play opportunities for children. He invited us to provide him with briefings as we developed our evidence base and policy proposals. It was therefore not too much of surprise when, at the Conservative Party conference in October 2006, a part of his keynote speech seemed strangely familiar:

> As children get older, they need to be able to exercise, they need to be able to roam. They need to be able to feel excitement. But you know what has happened? The average area within which a child in Britain roams freely now has shrunk in one generation to a ninth of what it

used to be. We have just one acre of playground for our children for every 80 acres of golf courses. We mustn't be the party that just says "no ball games allowed".

A year later, in September 2007 – after an even higher profile Playday campaign, this time focusing on the diminishing opportunities for children to play in the streets where they live – a further open letter appeared in the *Telegraph*, again coordinated by Sue Palmer. This time it had our name on it too, and was more focused on the need for national play policy. Titled 'Let our children play', the letter (Abbs et al, 2007) – signed by 270 professionals, writers and academics – cited 'the marked decline over the last 15 years in children's play [...] particularly outdoor, unstructured, loosely supervised play' as a 'key factor' in the 'explosion in children's clinically diagnosable mental health problems,' citing research by NCH Action for Children, one of the UK's largest children's charities. The signatories wanted 'a wide-ranging and informed public dialogue about the intrinsic nature and value of play in children's healthy development' and a debate about 'how we might ensure its place at the heart of twenty-first-century childhood'.

Soon after that, David Willetts's office contacted us to ask for our informal contribution to his party's forthcoming child policy review, which had been ordered by David Cameron after the UNICEF (2007) report. The review was to be an inquiry into the quality of childhood in the UK, 'seeking ways to help youngsters enjoy vivid lives and everyday adventures'. Over the following weeks, Willetts's team liaised closely with our policy and research team and we met with Tim Loughton, the Shadow Children's Minister, who was working with Willetts on the review. We were more than happy, of course, to provide the Conservative team with as much evidence as we could muster about the need for a serious government play policy. Then, two days before it began, I was asked to attend the Conservative Party conference in Bournemouth, joining Sue Palmer at a session with David Willetts on the main conference platform. Given Willetts's status – not just as education spokesperson, but also as one of the Conservative Party's leading thinkers – this seemed like a significant breakthrough to the heart of the Tory policy machine. My message to the Tory faithful was the same as it had been to the government for several years – about the need for a wide-ranging, multifaceted national play strategy – but David Willetts's speech suggested that a Conservative approach would be somewhat narrower. A clue to the Tories' thinking about play was in the original announcement about the Childhood Review, which promised to look at 'how to lift the red tape surrounding growing up in 21st century Britain'.[1] The Tories' dislike of administration and regulation did not begin or end with Oliver Letwin's misplaced putdown of CPC; it now seemed that – rather than aiming to tackle the dominance of motor vehicles, the lack of investment in public play areas or a planning culture that paid little heed to the needs of children – bureaucracy was to be identified as the reason for 'shrinking childhoods' (Willetts, 2006). Excessive health and safety concerns and a litigious, risk-averse culture in public play provision was a main theme of a speech in which Willetts (2006) promised that a Conservative government would amend the Compensation Act, ask judges to exercise more common sense, and remove playgrounds from the remit of the Health and Safety Executive.

The full report of the Conservatives' Childhood Review was launched by party leader David Cameron in February, 2008, but it was noticeably short on substance and offered nothing of the strategic approach that we had been advocating. At the launch, Cameron was clear that he did not see much of a role for central government. 'Above all,' he said, 'we need to understand that making Britain the most family-friendly country in the world is not just a job for the state, as Labour seem to think'.[2] The review itself did identify the imperative of 'making outdoor space safer and more protected, so that parents and children feel more confident about spending time there' (Conservative Party, 2008), but limited its response to this complex problem to an increase in community policing.

The economic crisis that was to change everything began, as far as the UK was concerned, with a run on the Northern Rock Building Society in August 2007 (House of Commons, 2008): three months before Ed Balls's Children's Plan statement to the House of Commons. The US sub-prime mortgage market – which had fuelled a housing boom but was underpinned by complex, opaque

---

[1] www.manchestereveningnews.co.uk/news/greater-manchester-news/tories-launch-childhood-review-986103

[2] http://news.bbc.co.uk/1/hi/uk_politics/7226514.stm

financial instruments that catastrophically undercalculated the risk of defaulting loans – had collapsed. The banks stopped lending to each other and this 'credit crunch' set off a chain of events leading to the worst recession since the 1930s.

Ironically the immediate effect of the crash on the Play Strategy was a further £10 million for the Playbuilder Programme, as Ed Balls – still one of Prime Minister Brown's closest allies – played his part in a short-term programme of 'quantitative easing': boosting the supply of money in the economy as a means to kick start its growth. Crisis-driven fiscal stimuli notwithstanding, however, the days of big government spending were over for the foreseeable future. The economic crisis and the bank bailouts in particular resulted in a level of government debt that ushered in a new era of austerity expected to last for at least a decade (Petrie, 2013). In these circumstance it was highly unlikely that further hundreds or even tens of millions of pounds of Treasury funding would have been made available for the second or third phases of the Play Strategy, as they had been for the first, whichever party (or, as it transpired, parties) was in power after the general election of 2010. However, it was not the new fiscal austerity per se that was to have such a terminal impact on England's Play Strategy so much as the political sea change that it prefaced.

David Cameron's Conservatives won enough seats to be the largest party in Parliament and could have formed a minority government. However, at a time of profound economic turbulence, it was argued that this would be reckless, risking a period of weak government and political instability that could endanger the recovery. So the Tories entered into discussions with the Liberal Democrats about forming a coalition government that would be a first in modern British politics. After a dramatic late flirtation with Labour – who many of their voters would have seen as more natural bedfellows – the Liberal Democrats made an agreement with the Conservatives (Boulton and Jones, 2013). On 11 May 2010, David Cameron formed a new coalition government with the Lib Dem leader, Nick Clegg as his deputy.

As the 2010 general election drew closer and the Labour government's tenure looked less and less secure in the wake of the financial crisis and Gordon Brown's difficult public image, Play England did its best to cultivate relations with the Conservative opposition and build on the links we had established through the Childhood Review. Several factors militated against this being as successful as we hoped. First, the financial crisis and the huge public deficit that it had left would mean that any new government would need to curtail public spending, and the politics of the economic arguments tended to place initiatives like the Play Strategy in the category of 'New Labour profligacy' as far as the Conservatives were concerned. Second, as the government's delivery partner for the Play Strategy, there was a sense that we were too closely associated with Labour, or at least their policies, for a Tory government to want to work with us. Finally, Michael Gove had replaced the relatively progressive David Willetts as Shadow Children's Secretary, a radical traditionalist who made no secret of his view that the government's role in children's lives should be limited to enabling schools to provide for their formal education (Gove, 2009).

One strong political connection that we made through the Childhood Review was with Tim Loughton, the Shadow Children's Minister, who had taken a keen interest in the potential for play policy and continued an occasional dialogue with us after it was published. In March 2010, speaking at the launch of our latest Demos report *People make play* (Beunderman, 2010) about the value and cost effectiveness of playwork and staffed play services, Loughton seemed to sense the anxiety of the sector, as public spending cuts loomed, when he acknowledged that 'it would be a false economy to cut these vital services'. This view was sadly not widely shared by his colleagues..

The logo of the DCSF was a rainbow and, in its more detailed version, the design included munchkin-like figures still constructing and painting it. This was a somewhat twee image, of course, with its clichéd allusion to 'building brighter futures together' almost a self-parody of tired government rhetoric around children. Yet, on one's less cynical days, the rainbow logo had brought a colourful and cheerful ambience to bear on the policy scene and we had learned to love it – not least at the DCSF main office in Sanctuary Buildings, Westminster, where a huge version of it hung imposingly over the large central atrium. A visitor to Sanctuary Buildings soon after the change of government that summer will have witnessed the giant rainbow being dismantled and the DCSF logos being removed from the windows and doors to be replaced by a plain and austere Department for Education sign in dark, civil service blue. It was the end of the rainbow, but there was no pot of gold.

On the DCSF website, too, the changes were swift and reflected the harsh nature of our new reality. 'This website is under reconstruction and may not reflect current government policy' was the large red warning sign that greeted visitors to the site that summer. Soon after, the guidance documents that we had produced for the Labour government were removed completely. The Play Strategy was over. In its place, at this stage, there was still the prospect of a new government play policy. We had agreed a smaller contract with the department to deliver a 'Big Society'[3] play programme, 'Engaging communities in play', which would explore, pilot and evaluate how local voluntary action could best support and promote children's play opportunities. The contract would only remain until the end of the current spending period, March 2011, but it would at least enable us to retain the best of our staff team and, more importantly, help the new government to formulate a longer term play policy that we could then help it to deliver. Or so we thought.

One of the new children's ministers at the Department for Education was the Liberal Democrat Sarah Teather. Speaking with her at an NCB event in June 2010, she said she was very interested in the play agenda and would like to meet with me in relation to a policy announcement that her leader Nick Clegg, the Deputy Prime Minister, would be making later that month. This would be a speech about the government's children and families policy in which Clegg (2010) announced a range of issues to be considered by a high level ministerial taskforce, chaired by the Prime Minister. Its agenda, he said, would include children's play:

> Every parent understands the importance of a secure
> environment for their children. Spaces where they
> can play, where they can feel completely free, where

---

[3]   The 'Big Society' was/is the name for an overarching Conservative Party policy launched by leader David Cameron in 2009, which posits increased volunteering and localism as the antithesis to the 'big state', theoretically maintaining important services whilst simultaneously reducing government expenditure on them.

they can safely push at the boundaries, learning and experimenting. Places where different generations can meet, binding the community together. We mustn't accept our playing fields being concreted over and our parks always being tucked out of public view. But if you ask adults if they used to play near their homes as children, 71% will tell you they did. Every single day. That compares to just 21% of children now. It's not right, and it has to change. (Clegg, 2010)

Like every English politician to speak about children's play during those years, the Deputy Prime Minister was, of course, quoting Play England research and adopting some of our rhetoric. After the trauma of the preceding weeks this was good news, even if the speech was highly qualified by the recognition of fiscal constraints: 'There's no more money to throw at these problems', he said, 'so we have to be innovative, we have to find new solutions [...] making it easier for volunteers and charities to get involved'. No new play strategy, then; but this clear reference from the Deputy Prime Minister to the work that we were about to begin under our hastily renegotiated government contract, and the involvement of the Prime Minister himself in looking at the policy implications of it, held out the prospect of at least a thread of continuity with what had been achieved, but really barely begun, under Labour.

The coalition government's first comprehensive spending review (HM Treasury, 2010b) brought that glimmer of hope for an emergent play policy to an end in one short sentence:

Overall resource savings in the Department for Education (DfE)'s non-schools budget of 12 per cent in real terms by 2014–15, contributing to overall DfE savings of 3 per cent in real terms [...] will be achieved by [...] rationalising and ending centrally directed programmes for children, young people and families.

This disproportionate contribution to the Treasury's longer term deficit reduction targets from DfE's non-schools budget spelled the end of national investment in play, at least for the first spending period of the new government. Even the original play contracts that had moved from DCMS to DCFS, and which dated back to the Thatcher government of the 1980s, were terminated. The invitation to meet with Sarah Teather never came, and the fate of Nick Clegg's task force became a Whitehall enigma, producing no reports (Kilkey et al, 2012) or even, it seems, ever meeting (O'Grady, 2011).

As for many other parts of the public and voluntary sectors, the coalition government years of 2010–15 saw severe reductions in services, spaces and projects for children's play. The Department of Health (2013) made £1 million available for Play England and partners to promote street play schemes similar to those described in our prologue, and Play England was also to play the lead role in a 'Big Society' initiative of the Cabinet Office, which saw around £2.9 million from its Social Action Fund shared among a range of national and local voluntary sector partners in the 'free-time consortium' (NCB, 2012). The aim was to increase the number of volunteers supporting children's play, and with 47,000 reportedly contributing after two years of the scheme, a further £900,000 was awarded after two years (Media Trust, 2013).

This superficially impressive figure could not disguise the fact that even armies of volunteers cannot, alone, sustain or replace public services. A report in the children's sector journal *Children and Young People Now* (*CYPN*) (Hayes, 2014) reported the results of a survey showing that capital and revenue spending on children's play by England's local authorities from 2010-13 fell by 50% and 61% respectively, representing a huge reduction in a form of year-round, mainly universal provision that could not be glossed over by counting the numbers of volunteers at an annual Playday, for example. A later Freedom of Information request by the Children's Rights Alliance for England (2014) found that almost 10% of the local authorities that could provide any information at all had actually reduced their play budget to zero for 2014–15. With the Local Government Association warning that more – and deeper – cuts, especially to non-statutory services, were to follow, this number looked certain to increase in 2015–16 and beyond, leaving the play movement in something of an existential crisis. Commenting on the *CYPN* report about the play cuts, Tim Gill (quoted in Hayes, 2014) summed up the new era for play policy as follows:

> 'These figures show just how fast England is moving away from the previous government's vision of outdoor play as an essential ingredient of a "good enough" childhood. The Play Strategy [...] accepted that central government had a lead role and invested widely in staffed and unstaffed facilities. Now [...] a growing number of children are being left with nowhere to play outdoors with their friends. Many will end up bored and stuck indoors – especially in disadvantaged areas, where parks, play areas and green spaces are often poor or non-existent, and where local authorities have historically invested in staffed facilities. Outdoor play remains on the public policy agenda – just [...] but these [government] initiatives in no way compensate for the decimation of local play facilities. It is hard to overstate the challenge now facing play advocates'.

The degree to which play policy was turned on its head in 2010–11 – and the perverse logic now at work within the public sector – was perhaps even better illustrated by a councillor's letter to the Brent Play Association after losing a long battle to retain the funding, or at least a title to the land, for the only adventure playground in this deprived London borough:

> The decision was made because the council had already ceased to fund play provision across the borough several years ago and this was the only remaining play scheme receiving funding. The funding of this project as a one-off was no longer sustainable when funding has to be prioritised for statutory services for children and older people. (From an email by Cllr. James Denselow, Cabinet Member for Stronger Communities, London Borough of Brent, to Brent Play Association, April, 2015)

In July 2015, just a few weeks after the Conservatives finally secured their majority at a general election for the first time since 1993, a demolition crew and bulldozers moved on to the site of the 36 year-old Stonebridge Park adventure playground. Some might say that the resulting dust and rubble was a suitable metaphor for their approach to play policy.

FOURTEEN

'Skylarks and canaries'

The legacy of the Play Strategy

At a meeting of Play England's strategic advisory group in 2010 – within the slender window of opportunity' between the termination of our central government contracts to support the Play Strategy (DCSF/DCMS, 2008b) and the conclusive elimination of children's play from government policy altogether, which would be confirmed by that autumn's comprehensive spending review (HM Treasury, 2010b) – Ryan Shorthouse, founder of the Conservative think tank Bright Blue and a key researcher for the shadow cabinet's child policy review three years earlier (Willetts, 2007), was addressing a somewhat shell shocked gathering.

The coalition government had made reducing government debt its 'most urgent task' (HM Treasury, 2010a), and reducing public expenditure the means to achieve it. The two parties agreed, as their basis for sharing power, 'that the days of big government are over; that centralisation and top-down control have proved a failure' (HM Treasury, 2010b). If Oliver Letwin's comments in 2004 had sounded ominous – for CPC and the many other specialist agencies holding government contracts to support particular policy areas – the subsequent economic crash of 2007–8 had presented the new government, for which he was now Minister of State for Policy, with its justification for following an agenda of deep cuts to public administration to a degree not previously imagined. That independent economists attributed the crash not to excessive government spending but to the recklessness of inadequately regulated financial markets (Farlow, 2013) did not deter them from pursuing such cuts with vigour.

The Play Strategy support contracts held by Play England and its partners were among the first casualties of the coalition's 'deficit reduction' programme. These were cancelled as part of the emergency budget announced by new Treasury Minister David Laws (HM Treasury, 2010a) less than two weeks into the new administration, in order that the restructured Department for Education could contribute £670 million to what were presented as 'efficiency savings' (HM Treasury, 2010a). The contracts had been due to run until 2011 and their sudden termination precipitated a major restructuring of Play England's staff, including many redundancies. External members of the advisory group that day in July were also considering an insecure future, as their own services and organisations began to take stock of a landscape that had changed beyond recognition.

Nevertheless, Nick Clegg's (2010) speech in June, as well as direct intimations from the new children's ministers from each party (Tim Loughton of the Conservatives and Sarah Teather of the Liberal Democrats), had given us cause to believe that the new government would not abandon play altogether. At the time of the meeting with Shorthouse, we were in fact negotiating with officials for a new short-term contract to develop support for voluntary and community play provision (Greatorex, 2011) as a small part of Prime Minister Cameron's vision for a 'Big Society'. What we needed to do, in order to make a convincing case for new play policy, said Shorthouse, was develop and present a persuasive evidence base. Leaving aside that the upheavals and gaps resulting from our massive unplanned loss of contract income[1] made research and policy development as difficult as all other aspects of the work over that period, this advice was met with a certain amount of grim irony from our members and colleagues around the table, who knew that probably the best opportunity ever to garner evidence to inform play policy was disappearing with the termination of the Play Strategy (DCSF, 2008) just a month earlier.

---

[1] Legally the government could have been held in breach of contract, but NCB, Play England's parent body – like the many other agencies in similar circumstances – did not consider litigation to be an option for fear of it compromising the pursuit of policy objectives with the new government.

Although the Play Strategy was a 10–12 year plan, a crucial part of the investment of £235 million for its first three years (2008–11) was, by definition, to research the impact of a public policy initiative for play. The Play Pathfinder programme – over and above the Playbuilder programme for 3,500 new play areas – commissioned just 30 local authorities in England to find the most effective ways to enable more children to play more often within a public realm more sensitive and responsive to their needs. This programme was to have been the subject of a major national evaluation, the results of which would have informed future play policy and investment decisions not only for the national government but also for the remaining 125 top-tier and 200 second-tier authorities in England. This evaluation – the 'evidence base' so valued by policymakers of every hue, not just bright blue – we felt confident would demonstrate beyond further argument that good play provision, and a wider planning framework that understood and responded to children as stakeholders in public space, should be an essential component of every community plan and every spatial development strategy, as well as integral to services that truly aimed to support the wellbeing of every child (HM Treasury, 2003). By July 2010, like every other part of the Play Strategy, this prospect was in tatters, the evaluation contracts cancelled like all the others.

In the event, it is unlikely that any amount of evidence would have dissuaded the coalition government in 2010 from divesting itself of responsibility for children's play. David Willett's policy review had led to little more than David Cameron (2007) echoing his elegiac reference to modern children needing the sort of 'everyday adventures' that his generation had enjoyed, without any suggestion of how his government would help. We now knew that it would not.

Writing about the impact of the Play Strategy, *The Times* journalist Damon Syson (2010) urged the government not to 'axe' the funding for what he called 'the play revolution'. Echoing the review by Frank Dobson, which had set the ball rolling back in 2002, he wrote that it was 'time to take play seriously' and that the new concepts and designs for public play areas that had proliferated under the Play Strategy – guided by the principles in *Design for play* and *Managing risk in play provision* – encouraged imagination and adventure, affording children more opportunity to take risks and have fun than the typical municipal playgrounds they were replacing. In truth, the Playbuilder programme – the only part of the twelve-year strategy to have been more or less completed before the new government abandoned it – was hardly a revolution. This was journalistic hype, but perhaps also evidence that the growth and change in public play provision brought about by the investment had made a big impression. Many of the new spaces redefined not only what a fixed equipment playground looks like but also what it offers to children. This was not just a superficial change, but also a result of the new approaches to design and risk management.

Just two days earlier, the same newspaper (Sugden, 2010) reported that 'parents have attacked a decision to scrap plans for hundreds of local playgrounds because of government spending cuts'. This was no hype. One of these parents, Emma Kane, who had been involved with her own children in the consultation for a new play area in their village of Hook Norton in Oxfordshire, had organised a national campaign: 'Save Our Playgrounds'. Petitioning the Prime Minister with over 1,650 signatures, she was quoted as saying: 'it's insane to cut what is such a small amount of money. There's a lot of disappointed children out there'. During the months of uncertainty that followed Michael Gove's decision to freeze the Playbuilder funding (pending a review of the 1,300 or so sites still to be built during the final year of the programme) Emma became something of a celebrity in the play sector, addressing meetings and conferences as the voice of parents who knew the real value, not just the cost, of good local play provision. How much impact this campaign had on the final decision is impossible to gauge, as is the number of sites eventually abandoned. Play England's monitoring role was terminated in June 2010, but our understanding from DfE officials was that around 22% of the funding for the final round was not paid, equating to approximately 290 sites. However, as part of the government's wider decision to remove the ringfencing for all non-statutory local authority funding, councils were at liberty to abandon their Playbuilder plans even for the remaining 78% of funding for the final round. There is anecdotal evidence that this happened only rarely, as most of the funding had already been committed, through the lengthy procurement process, before the government freeze, but the final number of new sites will probably never be known – only that it is reasonable to estimate a figure in excess of 3,000.

A more qualitative assessment of the Play Strategy – even those parts of it that were largely completed, like Playbuilder, before it was abandoned – is also difficult to make. The independent evaluation that was commissioned by the Labour government in 2008 was cancelled at the same time as Play England's contracts, in June 2010. This evaluation was to be undertaken by a consortium of three universities, Ipsos MORI and the Office of National Statistics, led by the public policy research specialists, SQW. It was to have reflected the Labour government's intention to establish an evidence base for the second and third phases of the strategy, mainstreaming the lessons and good practice established by the Pathfinder programme in particular, so that the road map set out in the guidance document *Embedding the Play Strategy* (DCSF, 2010) would have a solid basis of experience to draw on for the long-term mission to transform England into a country where all communities welcomed and respected children's play. This was one of the key tasks of the evaluation team: to provide information on how the programme was being implemented by the pathfinder authorities and to find and report on examples of good practice 'to inform further development of play policy and spending plans by local authorities and government' (SQW, 2013). In the event, as SQW's interim report (Frearson et al, 2013) admits, 'there are no findings on the impact that has been achieved by the programme'. Nevertheless, the curtailed evaluation report does offer a snapshot of how the aims of the Play Strategy were taking shape over its crucial first two years, and of how communities were responding.

A key long-term aim of the strategy was to bring about a change in attitude to children's play in the pervading culture and ethos within which policy and spending decisions affecting the public realm are made. It was a specific objective that local authorities and their communities should begin to afford children's play higher priority, greater recognition and more respect. This would mean local authorities assessing play needs through audits and by consulting with and listening to children, and then planning strategically and holistically how to meet these needs. Here, the evidence suggests that the agenda was being taken seriously and that the Pathfinder authorities were embracing the aims of the strategy quite vigorously. The interim SQW evaluation, through its baseline case studies of the Pathfinder authorities, found that they were all, for example, conducting 'some kind of mapping of play spaces in their area [...] regarded establishing strong strategic links with internal local authority departments as being essential to securing the long-term future for play', and were implementing 'a risk-benefit approach to risk management rather than trying to eliminate risk altogether'.

There seems little doubt that the Play Strategy was a popular policy with children and families, delivering direct improvements to the prescribed play spaces for millions of children. The SQW evaluation report found that 'most Pathfinders reported greater use of developed play areas than before [...] [with] anecdotal evidence from parents and local residents abut how much children are enjoying the new or refurbished sites.' This confirmed the more direct evidence of the government's own measure, National Indicator 199 (NI199), which was a survey of primary school children's level of satisfaction with their local parks and play areas. We had doggedly pursued the introduction of a national indicator for children's play for many years, primarily because departmental budgets followed them and we saw this as a key to unlocking funding. Very simply, local authorities opting to include the indicator in their Local Area Agreements – a mechanism for determining the level of central government funding for local authorities – would continue to receive treasury money for play according to their performance against the indicator.

According to the government's own national schools survey (Chamberlain et al, 2010), in the only year that NI199 was measured before the change of government there was an almost 8% increase in the numbers of children in England either satisfied or very satisfied with their local play offer. This may seem like a modest rise, but these indicators are notoriously hard to shift at all in the right direction. An 8% improvement in just one year (across the entire population of the relevant age group) surpassed all expectations.

The success of the Playbuilder programme – as evidenced by the National Indicator along with a positive evaluation – would have almost guaranteed further investment had it not been for the financial crash and the political earthquake that followed, but the parts of the strategy that were designed to bring about more profound and longlasting changes had either not properly begun, or had not yet had time to take effect. It is reasonable to project that these changes would, if the early momentum of the Play Strategy had been maintained for the remaining ten years, embedded a truly child-friendly approach to spatial development, urban planning, policing and traffic management, transforming the built environments and open spaces of the towns, cities and suburbs of England. The Play Strategy would have brought children back out onto the streets, repopulating and reanimating our public places in a way that has been lost from much of the country.

Tim Gill aptly described the trajectory of play policy in England over the first decade of the new millennium as the 'play sector rollercoaster' (Gill, 2015). Between 2000 and 2010, the combined central government and national lottery annual budgets for children's play increased from approximately £400,000 in 2000–1 to something close to £120 million in 2009–10. From 2006 to 2010, a total of £390 million of central funding was committed to play provision in England, compared with less than £3 million in the four years since.

The rationale for a national play strategy was not to make provision and space for children's play dependent on central funding. On the contrary, it was to raise the profile of play, highlight its importance and increase the level of knowledge and understanding of how to plan and provide for it at a local level. Ultimately, it was to elevate the status of play within local planning and spending cycles so that its provision would be commonly recognised as a priority and routinely afforded the sort of resources from within local authority budgets that initially were only possible because of the national programmes.

How Ed Balls came to the same conclusion is not recorded, except for the verbal report of a key civil servant working with him at the time. He related that, after his latest briefing to the Secretary of State, during the research for the Children's Plan, had still not suggested one specific play intervention over another as suitable for government policy (from a wide range of possible options), Balls simply looked up and said, 'we're going to need a strategy'.

The complexity theorist and playwork trainer Arthur Battram has a nice metaphor for policymaking, which he calls 'skylarks and canaries' (Battram, 2012). Societies, he posits – and governments in particular – come to important decisions by two different routes. In the first approach, the prevalence of skylarks – known by environmental scientists to thrive only when a certain number of ecological criteria are met – is taken as a proxy indicator for a desirable state of biodiversity. A healthy skylark population would be seen as evidence of a more generally thriving wildlife. Measures that increase the skylark population are taken to be good for the environment in general. In the second approach, it is well known that until as recently as 1986, canaries were used in coalmines to indicate the presence of poisonous gases which might be otherwise undetectable. A dead canary in the cage was an indication of danger and the need to quickly change course or retreat. In Battram's thesis, policy responses to 'dead canaries' are more common than the 'skylark' approach. The analogy is deliberately simplistic to make a point, but the nature of democratic politics and its relationship via a voracious media with moral panics and perceived crises does tend to mean that policy is generally made not according to long-term visions for, say, an empowered, healthy populace and the conditions that would engender such a state, but in reaction to the problems that seem most pressing or receive the most (and most negative) headlines.

A good illustration of 'dead canary' policymaking is the response to childhood obesity. A skylark approach to children's health would not focus on their weight at all, but simply envisage environments that we know to provide optimum opportunities for healthful activity and wholesome diets and set about providing them as widely as possible. This would, of course, include an abundance of opportunities for children to play. Playing children fully expressing their mercurial natures, using their bodies to explore and navigate their limitless worlds of imagination and form would get exactly the exercise they need. The canary approach directs overweight children to sports and fitness programmes that they already find difficult, while making them sit still and stand or walk in straight lanes for much of the rest of their day.

The challenge for play advocates is to engage with existing policy while keeping our own agenda clearly in focus. We do this by being clear that whatever benefits accrue from playing – to children's emotional health, capacity to learn, physical fitness, environmental sensibility or anything else – happen precisely because at play they are self-directed, making choices, dealing with cause and effect, managing risks and negotiating relationships: being responsible, in short, for their own experience.

Perhaps Ed Balls was an intuitive 'skylarker'. Perhaps, as an economist, he knew better than most how a range of different interventions, carefully coordinated, can make more of a difference to the long-term result than focusing efforts on one immediate problem, however pressing. It may be that, as a new parent, he had opened his eyes to the child's perspective of the world and saw that it needed improving – not just for the many children with specific needs, but also for childhood in general. Or perhaps he realised that children's play, far from being insignificant, is a central, fundamental part of how we live and that making space for it is a key to the well-being of society as a whole. Maybe as the new children's (no longer just education) secretary he was simply in a position to act with a broader remit than any of his successors.

Whatever the Secretary of State's motivation, the Play Strategy for England was the most wide-ranging and ambitious plan for children's play ever produced by a national government. Although the original focus and most of the attention it received was on its three-year building programme for 3,500 new play areas and 30 staffed adventure playgrounds, the strategy's innovation, and its real ambition, lay in aiming to change the planning and decision making frameworks for local government so that provision for children's play would become a bigger priority for both spatial development and children's services. Local play strategies, driven by crosscutting play partnerships supported by specialist training and professional development, were to become integral parts of the joint planning and commissioning cycles for local areas (DCSF, 2010), with local authorities incentivised to include play within their plans by a new national indicator: a key mechanism by which local councils could qualify for a greater funding contribution from central government departments by helping to meet national priorities.

In the event, the new playgrounds and play areas became the Strategy's only tangible legacy. The longer-term vision had scarcely begun to manifest before it was dropped by the coalition government. Play policy was sacrificed, as Oliver Letwin's remarks in 2004 foreshadowed, on the altar of 'efficiency savings' to help pay down the huge government deficit created by the financial crash and subsequent bank bailouts of 2007. The new playgrounds and play spaces had been mostly built (or at least commissioned) before the change of government, but these austerity measures and those that followed at a local level ensured that the wider improvements remained agonisingly out of reach.

Play policy advocates are concerned not just with staffed playwork provision but also with the wider opportunities for children to play: in their streets, estates and neighbourhoods; their parks and open spaces; in and after school; on the routes to and from it, and in other public places. The diminution in children's freedom to play out unsupervised in the streets and estates of their local neighbourhood, or to knock on friends' doors and disappear together into the nearest park or woods, is an issue at least as complex as that of diverting resources into playwork services. Tackling the problem effectively not only calls for concerted action on a number of fronts, but also demands a reevaluation of some premises that society seems to hold dear.

Exploding the myths of 'stranger danger'; rethinking the balance of priorities between cars and pedestrians; recognising that antisocial behaviour is often a subjective phenomena; designing parks and open spaces for the multiplicity of ages that use them; seeing the stereotypical public playground for what it too often is: a convenience for adults – these are just some of the shifts in attitude needed for a public realm that would support children's play. Each of these issues competes for space within a different agenda. Planning; law and order; traffic and transport; economic growth; (adult) culture and leisure; health and safety, child protection – these are all long-established policy areas whose assumptions may need to change if children are to be afforded more time and space to play outside the home.

Underlying the entire issue is the question of power. Does society want to empower its children? Or is this less important than – perhaps even in opposition to – the real aim of moulding them to sustain the status quo? In emphasising the importance of preparing children for the future, are we in fact condemning them to it? These are big questions, but they need to be considered if we are to honestly appraise our record on play policy and see clearly how to improve it.

Examples of how children's play is a more significant issue for government than politicians tend to assume can be found in other areas too. Ministers seeking to extend the education continuum by introducing ever earlier ages for starting school may find themselves paradoxically opting for a 'play-based' curriculum for these early years. Public health officials wanting to encourage more children into sport to combat the childhood obesity epidemic may find that providing time and space for free play is a more effective approach to promoting physical activity for more children. Educational psychologists struggling to cope with the increase in children seeming to present with symptoms of stress, anxiety or poor concentration may find that diagnoses of attention deficit disorder are less helpful than assessing the extent of such children's freedom to move and express themselves through play.

Many play practitioners and theorists balk at these connections, wary of instrumental agendas (Lester and Russell, 2008) undermining the case for 'play for its own sake' and introducing contexts based only on confusion and ignorance about the nature of play itself. Some fear that this can only result in services and spaces that fail children by claiming to provide for play but actually doing something else. This is a real concern. Agendas other than play for children are everywhere: education; childcare; physical activity; crime prevention; poverty reduction; social cohesion; outdoor learning; access to nature; safeguarding – the list of apparently benign policy aims for children's wellbeing and future life chances in which play could be said to have a role is a long one. For play advocates, the problem is simple. Play is directed by the playing child, who may not want to be physically active, to learn anything in particular, to behave respectfully or to explore nature. Most children will of course want do all of those things during their play lives – in their own time and in their own way – but when the agenda has already been set for them, what priority is afforded to that choice?

The English Play Strategy is over, the long-term impact of the London play policy remains uncertain, and it is unlikely that more than a handful of the hundreds of local authority play strategies produced during the boom years of 2006–10 are now more than a dusty relic of better times. The impact of a deep recession, a radically conservative government policy for children, and the longer term forces of a socioeconomic system and children's services sector more invested in children's 'future life chances' than their present reality have meant that this leg of the journey has not ended well. In spite of the policy breakthroughs related here the movement itself, certainly in England, is weaker than it has been for many years.

The demise of the Play Strategy was a consequence of much larger forces; there was not much that the movement itself could have done differently to prevent it. In the wake of the worst financial crisis in 80 years, followed by a radical change of economic policy, the tsunami that hit the shores of the public and voluntary sectors from 2010-14 washed away many more and bigger sandcastles than ours. As the movement showed signs of regrouping around the time of the 2015 general election (Voce, 2015), there were indications of some solid foundations, still intact.

There is a commitment to the cause of making space for children to play that defines its advocates. This commitment − shared by millions of parents and others who know the fundamental importance of space for children to play − means that, regardless of government policy, local play strategies or the strength of national organisations, there will always be people organising, finding resources and making things happen. A mile-long hopscotch trail in the East End of London; an old-school adventure playground in Wales becoming an internet sensation; an initiative by parents in Bristol to stop the traffic and let their kids play in the street and this becoming a national campaign; an inner city local authority in London legally securing the land for its adventure playgrounds in perpetuity - these are examples of the continuing successes and achievements of the play movement in Britain.

But to reach all children − to become the norm rather than the exception − these kinds of initiative and countless others need the support of local, regional and national governments, and even then it will take many years and decades to achieve. Most politicians may not get it at first, if ever; but for play advocates, securing for children a proper consideration of their need for space and time to be themselves, follow their own culture, play their own games with their own friends in their own way − and for society to provide for that collectively so that it is secured for all children − is a lifelong mission for a better, more human world.

There is an irony in the fact that it was a financial crash that brought to a swift end a short period of social policy that bucked the trend of ever increasing pressures on children to attain and compete in order to take their place in the relentless pursuit of economic growth. As that growth slowly returns, what are the prospects for a renewal of interest in play policy?

FIFTEEN

'Children now'

Responding to children's right to play: conclusions and recommendations

The story of the Play Strategy for England, and our overview of some of the key ideas and research on children's play and how it is constrained in the modern world, suggests that no society that values human rights or wants a dynamic, sustainable economy can afford to neglect play. A public realm – space, services and culture – that supports the basic needs of all its people must treat the innate and expressed desire of all children to play with at least as much seriousness as it does their anticipated future needs as employable adults.

Indeed, the evidence strongly indicates that these needs are complementary. How, indeed, could they not be? If playing stimulates brain growth, adaptability and emotional intelligence; engenders resilience and creative initiative, develops the child's sense of self and relationship and enables him or her to practice assessing and navigating risk, how could it not be a fundamentally important aspect of the growth and development that will equip him or her to do well in life and be a valuable member of society? To ask whether children play because of the deferred benefits they seem to derive from it, or simply because it's the best fun they can have, is the wrong question. The 'play for its own sake' versus 'play for positive outcomes' argument is a false dichotomy. No child has ever played to improve their future life chances, but there is plenty of evidence to suggest that, in playing, they do just that. From a policy perspective, however, the distinction is crucial.

Although what we know about children's play does not in fact support the unquestionable assertion that it is or must always be 'self-directed or intrinsically motivated' (there is too much evidence of the transpersonal, communal nature of much playing for that statement to stand unchallenged), we also know that the optimum conditions for playing are those which support and respond to children's own initiative, provide them with resources and space to manipulate and explore and give them permission to be spontaneous and expressive. The real question to ask is to what extent our expenditure on services and spaces for children – and on housing, streets, parks and public spaces for their communities – affords them such opportunities.

A policy for children's play must aim to address the barriers and cultivate the opportunities for them to be free to follow their own playful nature within the bounds of our need for them to be also safe from serious harm (and there, often, is the rub). Creating and allowing children's space must be a fundamental component of any meaningful policy and strategy for their health, development and wellbeing, and part of any long-term vision for the public realm.

So, what are the specific policy measures needed to bring about this change? Each government, local and national, will need to assess the barriers to and opportunities for play within its own area, according to its specific powers and duties. There are, however, some general measures which, adopted according to the circumstances and needs of a given community or population, are recommended as the principles on which to develop specific policies and plans.

A cabinet minister for children

A prerequisite for the kind of changes that are needed, implicit in GC17, is a recognition at the top level of government that children's right to play is of equal significance to their wellbeing and future life chances as their other rights under the CRC. This is only likely to come about, as the experience of English play policy demonstrates, if the most senior minister with responsibility for child policy has a broader portfolio than education.

The brief elevation of children's play to the level of a serious policy issue in England occurred as a logical consequence of the eventual recognition by the UK government (in the Children Act

2004) that, if the state's responsibility to support all children is wider than their right to an education, then the network of universal provision for them must include more than schools.

Initially this extension was primarily into state-subsidised childcare, but the Play Strategy established the principle that simply extending the hours during which children are in supervised settings fell short of meeting the principle set down in Every Child Matters (2003): that children need and are entitled to be provided with space and opportunity to enjoy their free time; to play with their friends in spaces and environments designed and responsive to that need.

A vision of that breadth and ambition is unlikely to ever emerge as government policy without the sponsorship and leadership of a cabinet minister: a secretary of state not just for education, but for children.

A cross-departmental plan for play

Such is the ubiquity of children's play, and so diverse the factors that either constrain or support it within the public realm, that an effective play policy must engage with and coordinate changes to a wide range of domains and functions. Planning; architecture and landscape architecture; traffic; police; housing; parks; leisure and cultural services; schools and children's services, early years' and childcare provision, as well as play services themselves, each have a significant role in either inhibiting or enabling children's play.

Logically, then, the national government should produce and implement a long-term, cross-departmental national strategy to identify and effect the necessary changes to policy and practice within each of these areas, according to a common set of understandings about the nature of play and playable space. Contrary to the popular perception of the Play Strategy for England of 2008–10, this should not be primarily concerned with improving or increasing the number of fixed equipment play areas, but rather should focus on strategic interventions through the policy areas that impact on children's environments beyond the playground.

Planning policy

National policy and guidance should place a duty on planning authorities to ensure minimum qualitative and quantitative standards for children's play space in new developments, supported by good practice guidance for the creation of child-friendly public space within spatial development strategies, local development frameworks and relevant master plans (such as the Mayor of London, 2008).

Traffic management

Departments for transport and highways should collaborate with planning policy to calm traffic flow in residential areas and around children's transit routes, introducing 'shared space' streetscapes, 'Home Zones', pedestrian areas and play streets wherever possible, with lower (15 or 20mph) speed limits as the norm for residential streets not so designed or designated.

Playwork and playwork services

Evolving the built environment to better accommodate and support children's play will take decades. Many, perhaps most, children today would not see the benefits of a child-friendly approach to planning and traffic management even if it started in earnest tomorrow. Even with the wide adoption of concepts and designs for public space that supported children to play more outside and gave their parents the confidence to let them, there will remain in many communities an important role for dedicated play spaces.

The best of these are traditional adventure playgrounds, staffed by skilled playworkers. A national play strategy should review and evaluate the adventure playground network and introduce a long-term sustainable development plan for this valuable and unique form of provision. Professional playwork should be fully supported by government policies for workforce development, and playwork services should be fully recognised by the relevant registration and inspection regimes, whose criteria should be based on good playwork practice.

Playwork does not only happen in adventure playgrounds, however. Playwork practice can be effectively applied to street play projects and 'play ranger' schemes, where practitioners engage with children and support their play within neighbourhood, community and open spaces.

Childcare and extended services

Children should be able to play freely after school in whatever environment they find themselves. School-aged childcare, after-school clubs and 'extended services' should contain: a basic offer of playwork provision, appropriately staffed by qualified practitioners; enriched play environments, including a requirement for outdoor space, as identified by good playwork practice; greater parity between the status, terms and conditions of teachers, playworkers and childcare staff; and inspection against criteria, by inspectors, that recognises and is consistent with playwork theory and practice.

Cross-professional training

Experienced playwork practitioners are also often the best advocates for play beyond the playground. A crosscutting approach to play provision at a local level will depend for its efficacy not just on the commitment and coordinated efforts of the fullest range of relevant public realm professionals and officials but also on the knowledgeable input of those working most closely with children at play. A key to an effective local play strategy will be the proactive cultivation of a better, evidence-based understanding of children's play within the professional sectors that conceive, design, develop and manage public space, particularly in residential areas and the transit routes between homes and schools, sports and leisure centres, parks and other open spaces.

Statutory play duty on local authorities

The impact of the play sufficiency duty in Wales has yet to be authoritatively evaluated but, as an interviewee in Lester and Russell's (2013) early analysis found, 'everything that governments do has an impact on children's ability to take time and space for playing, including the design of public space and roads, institutional practices in places such as schools, practices that reproduce fears'. Their report found 'a sense of excitement' around the process and a 'collective wisdom' emerging through 'supportive and collaborative networks [...] within a community of practice of adults looking to support children's play'. The UK government should monitor this work and explore its potential for replication in England.

In the light of the unexpected Conservative victory at the general election in May 2015, these proposals now seem unlikely to come to fruition in England, and may become even less likely as the full extent of the implications of the election results become clear.

David Cameron and his chancellor George Osborne's project to 'balance the books' is intrinsically bound up with their vision of a much smaller state. They look set to preside over such a radical diminution of the public realm, such a break up of what is left of the universal networks and services to meet the common good (Meek, 2015), that the concept of universal public play provision – let alone child-friendly plans and designs for housing, streets and neighbourhoods – engendered and supported by national government policy, would appear to be a fading memory.

And yet, either side of the election, over the spring and summer of 2015, a working group of the All Party Parliamentary Group (APPG) on a Fit and Health Childhood, chaired by Baroness Floella Benjamin, met to consider play policy proposals to the new government. The APPG's broad report on children's health (APPG, 2014) began to make the case once again for the kind of expansive, crosscutting play policy that had been so embodied by the Play Strategy. Among an ambitious range of measures, it called for:

> a new legal duty on public health bodies to work with schools and local government to ensure that all children have access to suitable play opportunities, within close proximity to their home and at school; guidance on including play within Local Development Plans; and training and guidance in the enablement of free play for all professionals with responsibility for children, including Ofsted.

Most significantly, the APPG called for the statutory duty on local authorities in Wales to be extended to England, and suggested that such a range of measures should be coordinated by – yes – a new national play strategy.

Three years after the English Play Strategy's premature demise, the United Nations called on national governments to stop and stand back, to consider long and hard how they will – how they *must* – make space for children to play. The implications of GC17 are that modern society needs to reappraise children's play and how policy treats it, requiring a multifaceted, long-term, properly resourced vision and plan. The Play Strategy held out such a vision and contained such a plan. Using the very resources and machinery of government which had long seemed anathema to the play movement, it adopted principles and concepts from playwork and play advocacy that, given time, would have brought about a sea change in how children's own here-and-now experiences, culture and aspirations – not as future adults, but as children now – are considered and reflected in the public realm. These have not been lost.

Considered generically – removed from the specific context of English children's services and New Labour reforms – the Play Strategy offered a template and a road map for campaigners, advocates and governments to effectively address the agenda laid out by the UN in its General Comment. It shows how a strategic crosscutting approach, perhaps underpinned by appropriate legislation and applied consistently to different levels of government, can halt the trend of shrinking childhoods, again freeing up space for children to be children in a world that protects and supports their right to play. Perhaps this is the Play Strategy's real legacy. Perhaps its work has just begun.

Epilogue

The actor, producer and former children's TV presenter Floella Benjamin, now Baroness Benjamin OBE of Beckenham, rises to speak in the House of Lords, where she is a member for the Liberal Democratic Party. The Baroness, familiar to everyone of a certain age from her time on *Playschool*, the BBC's iconic daily programme for pre-schoolers in the 1970s and 1980s, asks Lord Nash, a junior Education Minister in the new Conservative government, about nutrition in schools. She is rewarded with the promise of a new 'national obesity framework' by the end of the year and a meeting with the Minister to discuss what it should contain.

It is a mark of the very different world we now inhabit compared with the one of 2007 – when the Play Strategy was announced with a £225 million flourish by Ed Balls in the House of Commons – that this brief exchange about school food between two minor politicians in the upper chamber may represent the best opportunity for progressing policy for play in England over the course of the new Parliament. The general election of 7 May 2015 not only saw Ed Balls's Labour party spectacularly fail to return to government in the face of an unexpected Conservative majority, but he himself lose his seat in Parliament altogether. If the result was widely regarded as a shock, this was nowhere more true than within the play movement, where there was a reasonable hope – if not quite an expectation – that our strongest political champion of recent years, far from leaving politics altogether, as he has subsequently announced, would be the new Chancellor of the Exchequer and might be persuaded to resurrect his vision for a child-friendly public realm supported by a long-term strategic government policy for play.

It was not to be. The leading party of a coalition government that, as CRAE (2015) asserts, 'undermined children's rights under Article 31 by abandoning a ten-year national play strategy (and) [...] breaking a public commitment to develop an alternative cabinet-led approach to play policy', now had a mandate to pursue its low-tax, low-intervention vision of a minimalist state unencumbered by centrist partners. Children's play is unlikely to feature in its plans. Unless...

The significance of Baroness Benjamin's intervention was that, as the chair of the APPG on a Fit and Healthy Childhood, she is leading the cross-party backbench calls for the government to take a more proactive role in tackling the public health challenge of the obesity epidemic with an holistic approach that includes making more space and time for children to play. To further substantiate its calls for a new statutory play provision duty on local authorities, the APPG established a working group on the issue of children's play, to report in the summer of 2015. With the Department for Education still resolutely disinterested in much beyond the classroom the promised obesity framework now seemed to be the best opportunity to develop any kind of national play policy, and the public health commissioners now situated within local authorities the likeliest source of new funding for play projects.

Some three years before his casual traducement of CPC on the Today programme, Oliver Letwin was the Shadow Home Secretary: the opposition spokesman not on cutting the 'waste' from government spending, but on law and order. One of Prime Minister Tony Blair's more memorable soundbites was about being 'tough on crime, tough on the causes of crime' and, in what was seen as a departure from the traditional Tory approach to the subject, Letwin said in response that it wasn't enough to be tough on crime, or even the causes of crime, but that government needed to nurture and cultivate its opposite, which he called the 'neighbourly society' (Travis, 2002). 'At its simplest,' he said:

> this means making neighbourhoods safe for children to play in. More trusting than adults, children may be the first to recolonise the shared spaces of safer neighbourhoods. But then parents may gather round their playing children and start chatting among themselves, perhaps keeping an eye on each other's children [...] This is the start of community. (Travis, 2002)

Juxtaposed with his later disregard for a body whose very existence was to research and promote an approach that would engender just such neighbourhoods, Letwin's words in 2002 illustrate both the challenge and the opportunity for advocates of play policy. On the one hand, our leaders are prone to thoughtlessly dismiss children's play in the abstract as inconsequential, beneath the serious business of 'real' social and economic policy. Yet, when considering issues affecting the actual lives of constituents, children's play may sometimes present itself as a central part of the solution: in this case, liveable public space, neighbourliness and a consequent reduction in crime.

Street play projects like the one described in our prologue are now being promoted with Department of Health funding, awarded on the basis of a study that found children are three to five times more active outdoors than indoors, and that the activity of children during street play translates to an additional ten minutes of moderate to vigorous physical activity per day (Page and Cooper, 2014). If they have any value to policymakers at all, it is that these projects can demonstrate their effectiveness in helping to reduce childhood obesity. To the much-reduced Play England and its partners who are managing the Street Play programme, it is not about obesity at all. More children playing outside, more often, in the common spaces of their local neighbourhoods, is an end in itself. Nevertheless, such is the paucity of interest in children's right to play within current political debate that the Children's Play Policy Forum felt the need to couch its 'four asks for play' of the incoming government, even before the election result was known, in terms of their instrumental use to other agendas like 'reducing neighbourhood conflict and the resulting pressure on police time' and 'test[ing] innovative community-based health and well-being initiatives'.[1]

The most likely one of these proposals to gain ground as far as government support is concerned would seem to be the street play programme already under way. Play England hopes that these occasional road closures will act as a catalyst to playing children: helping to transform their communities, bringing families together in the way that Oliver Letwin once predicted. Neighbourhoods will in turn become more child-friendly and more playable so that

---

[1]   http://policyforplay.com/category/news-release/

in time, perhaps, there will be no need for the special permissions or the high-vis jackets.

That the modern renaissance of the street play movement originated not with government policy but with parents taking their own initiative (Playing Out, 2013) gives grounds for hope that it is an idea that can continue to grow, but with barely 250 schemes currently registered in a country with an estimated 12 million children it will need more support than the current £1.1 million over three years ending in March 2016. It must be hoped that Baroness Benjamin's famous enthusiasm will rub off on ministers, but with her party no longer in government and the anti-obesity lobby so preoccupied with nutrition and sport, the more ambitious demands of her APPG – even with the potential support of the new Children's Commissioner, the play movement's old friend Anne Longfield – seem unlikely to gain much traction in the era of endless austerity. Meanwhile the playwork field, facing something of an existential crisis in the face of the deep and continuing cuts, was attempting to regroup, with overwhelming support – albeit from a small survey – for the formation of a new vehicle to take on the challenges ahead (Voce, 2015).

Oblivious, children, of course, continue to play as they always have: adopting whatever is available to them, indoors or out, and making it their own.

> In the living room of a Victorian terraced house, in a street too close to a busy road and in an area with too high a crime rate for parents to feel confident to let their primary school children play out unsupervised, two brothers are huddled together over a computer screen laughing and talking with a third who has joined them via Skype from a different city. They are playing a game together on their respective screens, also connected by the internet. It involves an infinite number of loose parts that can be manipulated and shaped into boundless structures, the player's imagination the only limit. The children inhabit these virtual worlds they have constructed through playful avatars and interact with one another – and many other players – in treasure hunts, survival quests and all manor of mayhem and mischief. They are fully engaged in the game, which puts them in control, but also with each other: sharing tactics, ideas and experiments with the

functions and possibilities the game offers, frequently dissolving into laughter at unexpected consequences or the subversion of their plans by other players.

When the game is over, the Skype session curtailed not by waning interest but the need for a bath and some sleep, a parent asks the boys: 'What's the point of Minecraft anyway?'

'It's a game, Dad,' the older boy replies. 'The best game ever. You might as well ask, "what's the point of life?"'

References

AA Motoring Trust, 2014, Facts about road accidents, www.theaa. com

Abbs, P et al, 2006, Modern life leads to more depression among children, *The Daily Telegraph*, 12 September

Abbs, P et al, 2007, Let our children play, *The Daily Telegraph*, 10 September.

Adler, F, 1908, The basis of the anti-child labor movement in the idea of American civilization, *Annals of the American Academy of Political and Social Science*, 32, 22, Child Labor and Social Progress. Proceedings of the Fourth Annual Meeting of the National Child Labor Committee pp. 1-3

Adonis, A, 2012, *Education, education, education: Reforming England's schools*, London: Biteback Publishing

Ainsworth, M D S, 1973, The development of infant–mother attachment, in B Cardwell and H Ricciuti (eds) *Review of child development research* (vol 3), Chicago: University of Chicago Press, 1-94

APPG (The All Party Parliamentary Group on A Fit and Healthy Childhood), 2014, *Healthy patterns for healthy families: Removing the hurdles to a healthy family*, London: The All Party Parliamentary Group on A Fit and Healthy Childhood

Baldwin, J Mark, 1896, A new factor in evolution, *The American Naturalist*, 30, 354, 441–51, www.brocku.ca/MeadProject/Baldwin/Baldwin_1896_h.html

Ball, D J, 2015, Observations on impact attenuation criteria for playground surfacing, London: Centre for Decision Analysis and Risk Management, Middlesex University

Ball, D, Gill, T and Spiegel, B, 2008, *Managing risk in play provision, implementation guide* (1st edn), London: Crown Copyright/ National Children's Bureau/Big Lottery Fund

Barkow, J, Cosmides, L and Tooby, J (eds) 1992, *The adapted mind: Evolutionary psychology and the generation of culture*, New York: Oxford University Press

Battram, A, 2012, The PBI: 'Pink Bicycle Indicator' for play-friendly streets', [blog], https://plexity.wordpress.com/2012/01/09/play-friendly-streets-the-pbi-or-pink-bicycle-indicator-one-of-my-key-ideas/

BBC News, 2008, Ministers go swinging into action, 3 April

BBC News, 2013, Ramsgate girl's hopschotch grid 'sparked Kent Police warning', 9 May, www.bbc.co.uk/news/uk-england-kent-22475517

Bennett, A, 2012, 20 years since John Major's 1992 election: A retrospective, *The Huffington Post UK*, www.huffingtonpost.co.uk/2012/04/04/john-major-20th-anniversary-election

Bentley, T, 2003, *The adaptive state: Strategies for personalising the public realm*, London: Demos

Beunderman, J, Hannon, C and Bradwell, P, 2007, *Seen and heard: Reclaiming the public realm with children and young people*, London: Demos

Beunderman, J, 2010, *People make play*, London: Demos/Play England

Big Lottery Fund (BIG), 2005, Children's play initiative, www.biglotteryfund.org.uk/global-content/programmes/england/childrens-play

Big Lottery Fund (BIG), 2008, *Green spaces and sustainable communities*, final report to BIG from Sally Downs Associates in collaboration with Alison Millward Associates, London: Big Lottery Fund

BIG, 2009, Big Thinking - strategic framework, London: Big Lottery Fund.

Blair, C, 2003, Speech at the launch of Making the Case for a Children's Rights Commissioner for England, London: Houses of Parliament

Blair, T, 1993, *On the record* [radio] BBC2, 4 July.

Blake, W, 1789, *Songs of innocence and experience* (electronic edn, William Blake Archive, 2007), London: The British Museum

Blake, W, 1808, And did those feet in ancient times, in M Cox (ed), 2004, *The concise Oxford chronology of English Literature*, Oxford: Oxford University Press, 289

Boulton, A and Jones, J, 2013, *Hung together: The 2010 election and the coalition government*, London: Simon and Schuster

Bowlby, J, 1969, *Attachment and loss, vol 1: Loss*, New York: Basic Books

Brown, S, 1998, *Understanding youth and crime*, Buckingham: Open University Press

Brown, M, 2001, Welcome to the ministry of fun, Tessa, *The Guardian*, 11 June,

Brown, F, 2015, Play and playwork: stories of children playing, talk at Towards Play Sufficiency Research conference, Wrexham, Wales, 11 May

Brown, F, and Patte, M, 2013, *Rethinking children's play*, London: Bloomsbury Academic

Brown, F, with M King and B Tawil, 2007, *The Venture: A case study of an adventure playground*, Cardiff: Play Wales

Burghardt, GM, 2005, *The genesis of animal play: Testing the limits*, Cambridge, MA: The MIT Press

Butler, P, 2003, Livingstone judged most influential figure in Britain's public services, *The Guardian*, 10 September

Cameron, D, 2007, *Making Britain the best place in the world for children to grow up*, speech to launch More Ball Games, reported by The Guardian, 4 February

Campbell, R, 2004, Independence, at any cost, *The Guardian*, 5 November

Casey, T and McConaghy, R, 2014 The importance of access to play in situations of crisis, 18 June, [blog], www.ipaworld.org

Chamberlain, T, George, N, Golden, S, Walker, F and Benton, T, 2010, *Tellus4 national report: Omnibus/Panel survey for DfE*, DCSF Research Report 218, London: DCSF

Chief Medical Officer, 2013, *Our children deserve better: Prevention pays*, annual report, London: Department of Health

Children's Commissioner, 2015, *Why rights matter: The United Nations Convention on the Rights of the Child and the work of the Children's Commissioner for England*, www.childrenscommissioner. gov.uk/learn-more/takeover-challenge

Children's Play Council (CPC), 1998, *The new charter for children's play*, London: The Children's Society

Children's Play Council (CPC) / National Playing Fields Association (NPFA) / Playlink, 2000, *Best play: What play provision should do for children*, London: NPFA

Children's Rights Alliance for England (CRAE), 2014 *State of children's rights in England: Review of government action on United Nations' recommendations for strengthening children's rights in the UK*, London: CRAE

Children's Rights Alliance for England (CRAE), 2015, *UK implementation of the Convention On The Rights Of The Child: Civil society alternative report to the Committee on the Rights of the Child, England*, London: CRAE

Clegg, N, 2010, Supporting families and children, Barnardo's Lecture Series, 17 June, London

Cole-Hamilton, I, and Gill, T, 2002, *Making the case for play*, London: Children's Play Council

Cole-Hamilton, I, Harrop, A and Street, C, 2002, *Making the case for play: Gathering the evidence*, London: Children's Play Council

Cole-Hamilton, I, Greatorex, P, Jones, G, Croney, L and Prisk, C, 2009, *Better Places to play through planning*, London: Play England

Committee on the Rights of the Child (CRC), 2013, Article 31: General comment no. 17 on the right of the child to rest, leisure, play, recreational activities, cultural life and the arts, Adopted 17 April 2013, www2.ohchr.org/english/bodies/crc/docs/GC/CRC-C-GC-17_en.doc

Conservative Party, 1992, *General election manifesto: The best future for Britain*, London: The Conservative Party

Conservative Party, 2008, More ball games: the Childhood Review, Working Paper no 2, London: The Conservative Party

Conway, M and Farley, T, 2001, *Quality in play: Quality assurance for staffed play provision*, London: London Play

Cranwell, K, 2009a, Adventure playgrounds, in R P Carlisle (ed), *Encyclopedia of play in today's society* (vol 1), Los Angeles: Sage, 11-12.

Cranwell, K, 2009b, (Play in the) United Kingdom, in R P Carlisle (ed), *Encyclopedia of play in today's society* (vol 2), Los Angeles: Sage

Crewe, I, 1993, A nation of liars? Opinion polls and the 1992 election, *Market Research Society*, 35, 4,

Cunningham, H, 2007, *The invention of childhood*, London: BBC Books

Curtis, P, 2004, Extended schools criticised as 'boarding without beds', *The Guardian*, 8 September

CYPU (Children and Young People's Unit), 2001, *Building a strategy for children and young people: Consultation document*, London: Crown Copyright

Daily Telegraph, 2013, Police warned girl, 10, chalk hopscotch grid on path was criminal damage, *Daily Telegraph*, 9 May

de Coninck-Smith, N, 1999, *Natural play in natural surroundings: Urban childhood and playground planning in Denmark, c. 1930-1950*, Odense: Department of Contemporary Cultural Studies, The University of Southern Denmark

Department for Children, Schools and Families (DCSF), 2007, *The children's plan: Building brighter futures*, London: The Stationery Office

Department for Children, Schools and Families (DCSF), 2010, *Embedding the Play Strategy*, London: Crown Copyright

Department for Children, Schools and Families (DCSF) / Department for Culture, Media and Sport (DCMS), 2008a, *Fair play: A consultation on the Play Strategy*, London: Crown Copyright

Department for Children, Schools and Families (DCSF) / Department for Culture, Media and Sport (DCMS), 2008b, *The Play Strategy*, London: Crown Copyright

Department for Culture, Media and Sport (DCMS), 2003, *Getting serious about play*, London: Crown Copyright

Department for Culture, Media and Sport (DCMS), 2006, *Time for play: Encouraging greater play opportunities for children and young people*, London: Crown Copyright

Department of Health (DoH), 2013, Get active to get healthy [press release], 14 August, www.gov.uk/government/news/get-active-to-get-healthy

Dietz, W H, 2001, The obesity epidemic in young children, *British Medical Journal*, 322, 313-14

Dobson, F, 2006, Media release, London: Frank Dobson MP

Edwards, A, Barnes, M, Plewis, I and Morris, K, et al, 2006, *Working to prevent the social exclusion of children and young people: Final lessons from the national evaluation of the children's fund*, London: Department for Education and Skills

Evans, H, 1998, *The American century*, London: Jonathan Cape/ Pimlico

Fagen, R, 2005, Play, five gates of evolution, and paths to art, in McMahon, F, Lytle, D and Sutton-Smith, B (eds) *Play: An interdisciplinary synthesis,* Play and Culture Studies, vol 6, Lanham: University Press of America

Fagen, R, 2011, Play and development, in Pellegrini, A (ed), *The Oxford handbook of the development of play,* Oxford: Oxford University Press, 83-100

Farlow, A, 2013, *Crash and beyond: Causes and consequences of the global financial crisis,* Oxford: Oxford University Press

Ferguson, A, 2011, Playing out, www.playingout.net

Fortin, J, 2009, *Children's rights and the developing law,* London and Cambridge: Cambridge University Press

Frearson, M, Johnson, S and Clarke, C, 2013, *Play pathfinders evaluation: Interim report,* London: SQW/Department for Education

Furedi, F, 2002, Paranoid parenting: Why ignoring the experts may be best for your child, Chicago: Chicago Review Press

George, D L, 1926, in Brown, F and Patte, M, 2013, Rethinking children's play, London: Bloomsbury Academic

Geneva Declaration of the Rights of the Child, 1924, adopted 26 September, www.un-documents.net/gdrc1924.htm

Gill, T, 2004, Valedictory lecture at Children's Play Council, in M Frith, 'Battery-reared' children miss out on play, *The Independent,* 2 September, www.independent.co.uk/news/uk/this-britain/batteryreared-children-miss-out-on-play-6161080.html

Gill, T, 2007, *No fear: Growing up in a risk averse society,* London: Calouste Gulbenkian Foundation

Gill, T, 2008a, in Playing for keeps: interviews by Mary O'Hara, *The Guardian,* 9 April

Gill, T, 2008b, Play on, *The Guardian* online, 5 February, www.theguardian.com/commentisfree/2008/feb/05/playon

Gill, T, 2013, Seven principles of playground design, blog post, 20 February, www.rethinkingchildhood.com

Gill, T, 2014, *The play return: A review of the wider impact of play initiatives,* London: Children's Play Policy Forum

Gill, T, 2015, Play in the good times: the (English) inside story, *International Journal of Play,* 4, 3

Gleave, J, 2009, *Children's time to play: A literature review,* London: Play England, www.playday.org.uk/playday-campaigns

Gove, M, 2009, What is education for?, [speech] 30 June, London: The Royal Society for the Encouragement of Arts

Gray, P, 2015, *Free to learn*, New York: Basic Books

Greatorex, P, 2011, *Creating playful communities, lessons from the engaging communities in play programme*, London: Play England

Groos, K, 1901, *The play of man* (trans. by Elizabeth L. Baldwin), New York: Appleton, https://archive.org/details/playman00groogoog

Hayes, D, 2014, Play services decimated as funding slashed, *Children and Young People Now*, 8 January

Hillman, M, Adams, J and Whitelegg, J, 1990, *One false move*, London: Policy Studies Institute

Home Office, 2003, *Respect and responsibility: Taking a stand against anti-social behaviour*, London: Home Office

Hosken, A, 2008, *Ken: The ups and downs of Ken Livingstone*, London: Arcadia Books

House of Commons Treasury Committee, 2008, *The run on The Rock: HC 56-i, fifth report of session 2007-8*, London: Crown Copyright

HM Government, 2014, *The fifth periodic report to the UN Committee on the Rights of the Child*, London: Crown Copyright.

HM Treasury, 2003, *Every Child Matters*, London: Crown Copyright

HM Treasury, 2010a, *Budget: June 2010*, London: Crown Copyright

HM Treasury, 2010b, *Spending Review 41*, London: Crown Copyright

Hood, S, 2001 and 2004, *The state of London's children report*, London: Greater London Authority

House, R (ed), 2011, *Too much, too soon? Early learning and the erosion of childhood*, Stroud: Hawthorn Press

Hughes, B, 2001, *Evolutionary playwork*, London: Routledge

Hughes, B, 2003, Play deprivation, play bias and playwork practice, in Brown, F (ed), *Playwork: Theory and practice*, Buckingham: Open University Press

Hughes, B, 2005, National conference speech, reported in *Nursery World*, 15 June

Hughes, G, 2007, *The politics of crime and community*, Basingstoke: Palgrave

Hurtwood, Lady Allen of, 1968, *Planning for play*, London: Thames and Hudson

ICM Research, 2009, Make time for play: playday campaign, www. playday.org.uk/campaigns

International Association for the Child's Right to Play (IPA), 2013, UN stands up for children's right to play, arts and leisure in a landmark moment for children, [press release], 1 February, www.ipaworld.org

International Association for the Child's Right to Play (IPA), 2015, Is South Sudan about to ratify the CRC?, [press release], 26 January, www.ipaworld.org

Jacobs, J, 1961, *The death and life of great American cities*, New York: Vintage Books

Jefferson, T. et al, 1776, *Declaration of Independence, 4th July 1776*, Copy held at the Library of Congress, Washington, DC: The Thomas Jefferson Papers, Library of Congress

Jowell, T, 2005a, Response to the play review: letter to Frank Dobson MP, *Local Government Chronicle*, 20 January, www.lgcplus.com/response-to-childrens-play-review-published/560190.article

Jowell, T, 2005b, *Tackling the 'poverty of aspiration' through rebuilding the public realm*, London: Demos

Kane, P, 2004, *The play ethic: A manifesto for a different way of living*, London: Macmillan

Karsten, L and Van Vliet, W, 2006, Increasing children's freedom of movement: introduction, *Children, Youth and Environments*, 16, 1, 69-73

Kilkey, M, Ramia, G and Farnsworth, K, 2012, *Social policy review: Analysis and debate in social policy*, Bristol: Policy Press.

Klein, K, (1975) *The collected writings, volume 2 – the psychoanalysis of children*, London: Hogarth Press

Krappman, L, 2011, Presentation to the World Congress of the International Play Association, Cardiff, 7 July.

Labour Party, 2005, *Manifesto*, London: Labour Party

Lacey, L, 2007, *Street play: A literature review*, London: Play England

Laming, Lord, 2003) *The Victoria Climbié Inquiry: Report of an inquiry by Lord Laming*. London: Crown Copyright.

Lammy, D, 2007, Making space for children: the big challenge for our public realm, *Thinkpiece*, London: Compass

Lester, S and Maudsley, M, 2006, *Play, naturally: A review of children's natural play*, London: Children's Play Council

Lester, S and Russell, W, 2008, *Play for a change, play, policy and practice: A review of contemporary perspectives*, London: Play England

Lester, S and Russell, W, 2010, *Children's right to play: An examination of the importance of play in the lives of children worldwide*, Working papers in Early Childhood Development, 57, The Hague: Bernard Van Leer Foundation

Lester, S and Russell, W, 2013, *Leopard skin wellies, a top hat and a vacuum cleaner hose: An analysis of Wales's play sufficiency assessment duty*, Cardiff: Play Wales / University of Gloucestershire

Lindenmeyer, K, 1997, *A right to childhood: The U.S. Children's Bureau and child welfare, 1912-46*, Illinois: University of Illinois

Letwin, O, 2002, Speech to the Centre for Policy Studies, in *The neighbourly society: Collected speeches, 2001-2003*, London: Centre for Policy Studies, p10

Letwin, O, 2004, *Today* [radio], BBC Radio 4, 26 July

Livingstone, K, 2005, Speech at press conference on London terrorist bombings, 7 July, www.bbc.co.uk

Louv, R, 2005, *Last child in the woods*, New York: Algonquin Books

Mackett, R and Paskins, J, 2008, Children's physical activity: The contribution of playing and walking, *Children and Society*, 22, 345-7.

Major, J, 1999, How I gave hope to the poor, *New Statesman*, 8 November, .

Malkin, B, 2008, Politicians at play: Ed Balls and Andy Burnham go swinging, *Daily Telegraph*, 3 April

Marsh, I and Melville, G, 2006, *Crime, justice and the media*, London: Routledge

Mason, T, 2005, Jowell in 'u-turn' on play funding, *Third Sector*, 26 January

Matrix Evidence, 2010, *An economic evaluation of play provision: Final report*, London: Play England

Mayor of London, 2004a, *Making London better for all children and young people*, London: Greater London Authority

Mayor of London, 2004b, *The London plan: The spatial development strategy for London*, London: Greater London Authority

Mayor of London, 2005, *Guide to preparing local play strategies: Planning inclusive play space and opportunities for all London's children and young people*, London: Greater London Authority

Mayor of London, 2008, *Supplementary planning guidance: Providing for children and young people's play and informal recreation*, London: Greater London Authority

Mayor of London, 2015, *The London plan: The spatial development strategy for London, consolidated with alterations since 2011, Policy 3.6*, London: Greater London Authority

McAuley, C, 2010, *Child well-being: Understanding children's lives*, London: Jessica Kingsley Publishers

McKelway, A, 1913, Declaration of dependence by the children of America in mines and factories and workshops assembled, in H.D. Hindman, 2002, *Child labor: An American history*, New York: M. E. Sharpe,

Media Trust, 2013, Funding boost for play projects, 30 May, www.mediatrust.org/newswirefeed/funding-boost-for-play-projects/3823

Meek, J, 2015, Who will protect, provide, shelter, build? Why privatisation is the key to the election, *The Guardian*, 27 April,

Morris, K, Barnes, M, Mason, P, 2009, *Children, families and social exclusion: New approaches to prevention*, Bristol: Policy Press

Morrow, V, 2004, Children's 'social capital': implications for health and well-being, *Health Education*, 104, 4, 211-25

Moss, P and Petrie, P, 2002, *From children's services to children's spaces: Public policy, children and childhood*, London: Routledge Falmer

National Children's Bureau (NCB), 2012, Play England calls for community action to help children missing out on outdoor play [press release], 20 January, www.playengland.org.uk/news/2012/01/play-england-calls-for-community-action-to-help-children-missing-out-on-outdoor-play.aspx

National Union of Teachers (NUT), 2007, *Time to play: NUT play policy*, London: NUT

Nebelong, H, 2004, Nature's playground, *Green Places*, May, 28

New Statesman, 2010, Neil Kinnock, militant speech, Labour Party conference, October 1985, *New Statesman*, 4 February, www.newstatesman.com/uk-politics/2010/02/labour-militant-speech-kinnock

Newiss, G and Traynor, M, 2013, *Taken: A study of child abduction in the UK*, London: PACT and the Child Exploitation and Online Protection Centre

Nicholson, S, 1971, *The theory of loose parts – an important principle for design methodology*, London: Open University

Norman, N, 2004, *An architecture of play: A survey of London's adventure playgrounds*, London: Four Corners Books

NPFA (National Playing Fields Association), CPC (Children's Play Council) and Playlink, 2000, *Best play: What play provision should do for children*, www.playengland.org.uk/resources/best-play.aspx

O'Grady, S, 2011, Fiasco of Nick Clegg 'task force' to aid the family, *Daily Express*, 7 March, www.express.co.uk/news/uk/233011/Fiasco-of-Nick-Clegg-task-force-to-aid-the-family

O'Hara, M, 2008, Does the play strategy go far enough?, *The Guardian*, 9 April

Page, A and Cooper, A, 2014, *Outdoors and active: Delivering public health outcomes by increasing children's active travel and outdoor play*, Bristol: Centre for Exercise, Nutrition and Health Services, University of Bristol

Palmer, S, 2006, Toxic childhood: *How the modern world is damaging our children and what we can do about it*, London: Hachette UK

Pellegrini, A D, Dupuis, D and Smith, P K, 2006, Play in evolution and development, *Developmental Review*, 27, 261-76

Petrie, S, 2013, *Controversies in policy research: Critical analysis for a new era of austerity and privation*, London: Palgrave Macmillan

Piachaud, D and Sutherland, H, 2001, *Child poverty in Britain and the New Labour government*, London: London School of Economics

Piaget, J, 1951, *Play, dreams and imitation in childhood*, (trans. Gattegno and Hodgson), Abingdon: Routledge

Pilcher, J and Wagg, S, 1996, *Thatcher's children? Politics, childhood and society in the 1980s and 1990s*, London: Falmer Press

Play England, 2006, *The charter for children's play (revised)*, www.playengland.org.uk/media/71062/charter-for-childrens-play.pdf

Play England/ICM, 2009, Playday opinion poll summary, www.playday.org.uk/media/2634/playday_2009_opinion_poll_summary.pdf

Play England/IPSOS Mori, 2006, Playday opinion poll summary, www.playday.org.uk/media/2634/playday_2006_opinion_poll_summary.pdf

Play Safety Forum, 2002, repr 2008, *Managing risk in play provision: Position statement*, London: NCB for Play England

Playing Out, 2013, *Playing out story*, www.playingout.net/about/
playing-story/

PPSG (Playwork Principles Scrutiny Group), 2005, *The playwork
principles*, Cardiff: Play Wales/Skillsactive, www.skillsactive.com/
PDF/sectors/Playwork_Principles.pdf

Prout, A, 2005, *The future of childhood*, Abingdon: Routledge-Falmer

Raven, S, 1977, Treasure Islands, The Sunday Times colour
supplement, 7 August, reprinted by London Play, www.londonplay.
org.uk/resources/0000/1191/1977_Sunday_Times_colour_
supplement.pdf

Rawnsley, A, 2001, *Servants of the people: The inside story of New
Labour*, London: Penguin Books

Robinson, S, 2005, *Children's rights: Historic developments*, www.
cumberlandlodge.ac.uk/Programme/Resource+Library/
Young+People+Reports+children's lives

Roopnarine, J L, 2011, Cultural variations in beliefs about
play, parent–child play, and children's play: meaning for child
development, in A Pellegrini (ed), *The Oxford handbook of the
development of play*, Oxford: Oxford University Press

Schiller, F, [1794] 2012, *On the aesthetic education of man*, Mineola,
NY: Dover Publications

Schwartzman, H (ed), 1978, *The anthropology of children's play*, New
York, NY: Plenum Press

Seldon, A, 2007, *Blair unbound*, London: Simon and Schuster

Select Committee on Culture, Media and Sport, 2007, *Sixth Report*,
London, House of Commons

Shackell, A, Butler, N, Doyle, P and Ball, D, 2008, *Design for play: A
guide to creating successful play spaces*, London: DCSF/Play England

Shier, H, 1984, *Adventure playgrounds: An introduction*, London:
National Playing Fields Association

Shifrin, T, 2003, Lottery fund merger timetable unveiled, *The
Guardian*, 23 October,

Skenazy, L, 2009, *Free-range kids: Giving our children the freedom we
had without going nuts with worry*, San Francisco: John Wiley & Sons

Skillsactive, 2010, *National occupational standards for playwork*, www.
skillsactive.com/standards-quals/playwork

Smith, C, 2001, in M Conway and T Farley, Foreword, *Quality in
Play*, London: London Play,

Smith, P K, 2005, Social and pretend play in children, in A D Pellegrini and P K Smith (eds) *The nature of play: Great apes and humans*, London: The Guildford Press

Smith, F and Baker, J, 2000, *The childcare revolution: A decade of kids' clubs*, London: Brunel University College

Spencer, H, 1864, *The principles of biology*, London/Edinburgh: Williams and Norgate, https://archive.org/details/principles biolo05spengoog

Spiegel, B, 2011, Ripping up the rulebook, *Green Places*, June, 31-4

Spinka, M, Newberry, R and Bekoff, M, 2001, Mammalian play: training for the unexpected, *The Quarterly Review of Biology*, 76, 2, 141-68

Squires, P, 2008, *ASBO nation: The criminalisation of nuisance*, Bristol: Policy Press

Stobart, T (ed), 2001, *Take 10 for play* (5th edn), Gloucester: National Centre for Playwork Education, SW & Furzeham Publishing

SQW Consulting, 2013, Play Pathfinders and Play Builders Programme evaluation: Research report RR231, London: SQW.

Sugden, J, 2010, Parents attack plan to scrap playgrounds, *The Times*, 11 August,

Sutton-Smith, B, 1997, *The ambiguity of play*, Cambridge, MA: Harvard University Press

Sutton-Smith, B, 2003, Play as a parody of emotional vulnerability, in JL Roopnarine (ed) *Play and educational theory and practice, play and culture studies 5*, Westport, CT: Praeger

Syson, D, 2010, Bring on the years of living dangerously, *The Times*, August 13, *The National Lottery Bill 1992*, London: Crown Copyright

Thomas, G and Hocking, G, 2003, *Other people's children: Why their quality of life is our concern*, London: Demos

Torkildsen, G, 1996, *Supporting the children's play sector in London: Report to the London Boroughs Grants Committee*, London: London Boroughs Grants Committee

Torkildsen, G, 2012, *Leisure and recreation management*, London: Routledge

Travis, 2002, Letwin sees 'neighbourly society' as the way to beat crime, *The Guardian Online*, 9 January, www.theguardian.com/politics/2002/jan/09/uk.conservatives

Truss, L, Childcare minister Elizabeth Truss attacks unruly nurseries, *The Guardian Online*, 22 April, www.theguardian. com/education/2013/apr/22/childcare-minister-elizabeth-truss-nurseries

UK Parliament, 2004, Select committee on culture, media and sport fifth report,157-65, www.publications.parliament.uk/pa/cm200304/cmselect/cmcumeds/196/19611.htm

United Nations (UN), 1959, *General Assembly Resolution 1386 (XIV): Declaration of the Rights of the Child*, 20 November, www.un-documents.net/a14r1386.htm

United Nations Office of the High Commissioner for Human Rights, 1989, *Convention on the Rights of the Child*, www.ohchr.org/en/professionalinterest/pages/crc.aspx

United Nation Children's Fund (UNICEF), 2007, *Child poverty in perspective: An overview of child well-being in rich countries*, Florence: Unicef Innocenti Research Centre

Voce, A, 2001, In praise of Chris Smith, letter to *The Guardian*, 11 June, www.theguardian.com/theguardian/2001/jun/12/guardianletters

Voce, A (ed), 2006, *Planning for play: Guidance on the development and implementation of a local play strategy*, London: National Children's Bureau/Big Lottery Fund

Voce, A, 2007, All to play for, *The Guardian*, 31 July, www.theguardian.com/society/2007/jul/31/childrensservices.publicservices

Voce, A, 2008, Some room of their own, *The Guardian*, 3 April,

Voce, A, 2015, Advocating for play at the crossroads (part 1), [blog], www.policyforplay.com

Voce, A, 2015, *Playwork community says 'yes' to new vehicle*, www.policyforplay.com

Vygotsky, L S, 1967, Play and its role in the mental development of the child, *Soviet Psychology*, 5, 6–18

Ward, C, 1978, *Child in the city*, London: The Architectural Press Ltd

Webb, S and Brown, F, 2003, Playwork in adversity: working with abandoned children, in F Brown (ed), *Playwork: Theory and practice*, Buckingham: Open University Press

Welsh Assembly Government, 2002, *Play policy*, Cardiff: Crown copyright

Welsh Government, 2011, *The Rights of Children and Young Persons (Wales) Measure*, Cardiff: Welsh Government

White, M, 1999, PM's 20-year target to end poverty: Michael White on a high-profile attempt to show the government means business on welfare reform, *The Guardian*, 19 March

Wighton, D, 1998, *The Independent*, 23 October, http://blogs.independent.co.uk/2013/02/14/intensely-relaxed-about-people-getting-filthy-rich/

Wilby, P, 2007, Britain has lost the art of socialising the young, *The Guardian*, 1 August 2007

Wilkin, A, White, R and Kinder, K, 2003, *Towards extended schools: A literature review*, National Foundation for Educational Research, Research Report No. 432, London: DfES

Wilkinson, H, 1999, *Crèche barriers: How Britain can grow its childcare industry*, London: Demos

Wilkinson, H, 2001, *Crèche barriers: How Britain can grow its childcare industry*, London: Demos

Willetts, D, 2006, *Our children have a right to childhood*, http://conservative-speeches.sayit.mysociety.org/speech/599988

Williams, Z, 2006, *The commercialisation of childhood*, London: Compass, www.compassonline.org.uk

Winnicott, D W, 1964, *The child, the family, and the outside world*, London: Penguin Books

Winnicott, D W, 1971, *Playing and reality*, London and New York: Routledge Classics

Youlden, P and Harrison, S, 2006, *The better play programme, 2000-2005: An evaluation for Children's Play Council and Barnardo's*, London: Children's Play Council

Index

Index